D0343949

Roughnecks

Roughnecks

Tom McGregor

first choice

B XTREE

All photographs by Neil Genower and Rhuary Grant
except photograph on page 39 which is by Sven Arnstein

Published by Boxtree Limited, Broadwall House,
21 Broadwall, London SE1 9PL, 1995

10 9 8 7 6 5 4 3 2 1

A CIP catalogue entry for this book is available from the British Library.

ISBN: 0 7522 0736 9

Cover design by Design 23
Design by Dan Newman

Printed and bound in the United Kingdom by
Bath Colourbooks, Glasgow.

Contents

▲
Exploration
▼

'I thought, oh my God, I'm going to have to *climb* that. I nearly passed out at the prospect. Then I looked over to Charles. He had turned rather an unattractive colour ...'

So speaks Moira Williams, producer of 'Roughnecks', about the joys of researching locations in which to film one of the toughest and most challenging, yet most rewarding television series of her career. Anyone who thinks producing is all glamour and no grind should think again.

'We were about to board an oil rig docked in the Firth of Forth,' continues Moira. 'Until that point Charles and I had been helicoptered out to rigs, either landing on them or being lowered onto them. That was bad enough. This, however, was an entirely different kettle of fish – and a horribly daunting prospect. When you're approaching a docked rig from the land you get an entirely different perspective. There we were bobbing about in a tiny fishing boat and it's just this enormous structure in front of you with tiny little rungs going up the side of a vast pontoon. Those were the rungs that we thought we would have to climb.'

In the event, neither Moira nor Charles Elton, her co-producer at First Choice, had to climb up the structure. As they stood looking up at the towering edifice, a tyre with rope wrapped around it was slowly being lowered towards them from the deck of the rig. 'We had to climb onto the tyre,' continues Moira, half-laughing and half-grimacing at the memory. 'It was a case of hang on for dear life while they winch you up and just pray that it's not going to be too windy. It was at that moment,' she adds with feeling, 'that I swore our next production would be set entirely in the Paris Ritz.'

But they hadn't even started this production yet.

'Roughnecks', at that point, was barely more than an idea – an ambitious and potentially hazardous one at that. Why, with a world full of

Aerial view of the Osprey Explorer

Roughnecks

The camera crew

calm oceans and warm countries, did First Choice – a company with an international reputation for producing award-winning drama (last year it won a prize at Cannes and achieved an Oscar nomination) – decide to make a series set in the middle of the North Sea, one of the most uninviting, inhospitable corners of the globe?

Moira points out that it was Scotland in general and not the North Sea or the oil industry in particular that initially framed their decision. 'As someone who was brought up in Scotland, I was increasingly conscious that – until quite recently – Scotland got pretty short shrift in the television stakes. There wasn't much coming out of the country and anything that did originate there was invariably awash with English actors and English voices. Furthermore,' says Moira, pre-empting questions about Rab C. Nesbitt and Hamish Macbeth, 'there's been very little on the subject of how people rub along together in fairly confined spaces; it's a concept that fascinates me. I've always been very keen on that idea of ensemble pieces; of a large cast in a fairly static environment. It's always been in the back of my mind to base a series round it.'

It was a combination of circumstances that ultimately led to deciding on the oil industry. Like any other production company, First Choice receives a great deal of scripts and ideas, yet a wonderful idea does not always a good script make – and a good script can be short on ideas. 'We did,' says Moira, 'receive three or four manuscripts over the years featuring oil rigs and the industry, but none of them covered the ground we were most interested in.'

Yet Moira herself began to focus on the subject of oil and finally came to the logical conclusion that there was only one way to combine Scotland, a large cast, a confined space and that industry: put them on an oil rig. Once the idea was conceived, her enthusiasm – and Charles's – grew.

'We reckoned it would be a wonderful vehicle through which to concentrate on the group dynamics of ordinary lives,' says Charles. 'The last thing we wanted was to make a programme about men in suits banging their fists on boardroom tables – and banging on about the price of oil.'

First Choice wasn't the only company which recognized the idea as a viable proposition. ITEL, the distribution arm of Anglia TV (and the company that now distributes the series abroad), became interested and agreed to help fund research. Yet as soon as First Choice began to 'put the feelers out' within the oil industry, they met with resistance. 'I don't blame them,' says Moira, 'they'd had a difficult time with previous accident-led series and they assumed we were going to make a disaster movie.'

That, as Charles points out, was the last thing on their minds. 'It would have been ridiculous and unrealistic. It would be the same as doing a series about an airline and having planes crash every episode. It just doesn't happen.' Yet no-one at First Choice – unsurprisingly – knew exactly what *does* happen on an oil rig. Not many people do; and that was another attraction of the idea. Here was an industry that helps keep the UK economy afloat – yet few people know anything about it. Especially at grass-roots level.

After their initial treatment was prepared with a daunting lack of cooperation from the oil industry, Moira and Charles realised that they needed a good investigative journalist and scriptwriter if they were to pursue the project. Enter Kieran Prendiville. An investigative journalist and news reporter, he has worked on numerous major television series including 'Horizon', 'Tomorrow's World', 'Sportsnight', 'Grandstand' and 'Nationwide'. His more recent incarnation is as a scriptwriter and he has worked on 'The Bill', 'Boon', 'Making News' and 'Perfect Scoundrels'. In short, his experience made him the obvious candidate for researching and writing a drama series that would rely heavily on accuracy. Furthermore, he wasn't a stranger to First Choice: he and Charles had worked together on previous occasions.

Kieran was immediately taken by the idea and jumped at the opportunity to research into an industry about which, like the others, he knew almost nothing. As Charles says, 'Kieran's a terrific investigative journalist and is also brilliant at finding out about people's lives. Put him in a pub or anywhere and within five minutes he's best mates with everyone.'

Kieran, not sure whether or not he would get a positive response, contacted an old acquaintance who worked in the industry and told him he wanted to go out to an old rig. The response, remembers Kieran, was enthusiastic. 'He said, sure, we've got a rig spudding in: come up and look at it.'

To the uninitiated (including Kieran at that point) 'spudding in' sounds like a dubious activity, possibly not unrelated to potatoes. It is, in fact, oil-speak for drilling a hole.

So Kieran went north to look at the hole, leaving Charles and Moira in London, confident that he would be best mates with several riggers in no time.

'What on earth an I *doing* here?' Our intrepid researcher is standing on the deck of a rig in the freezing cold, huddled against the lashing rain and howling gales, looking out to sea (there's nowhere else to look). He is not a happy man. He will remain unhappy for a number of days.

'The thing about starting research is how lonely it is, particularly when you're on an oil rig on the edge of the Arctic Circle surrounded by people who are both rather suspicious of you and too busy to pay much attention to you.'

To alleviate the boredom, Kieran has started smoking again, which is a pity as he gave up only six months ago. But he's not the only one to resort to the evil weed: he's just met a man who had never smoked in his life until he went out onto this rig. 'His colleagues told him he wasn't allowed into the coffee shack (the hut on the rig where coffee breaks are taken) unless he smoked. Now he's on forty a day.'

Kieran himself decides to take refuge in the coffee shack. It's the most likely place to find people to talk to him, and apart from anything else, it's also quieter than being outside. If there is one thing Kieran has learned, it's that they won't be able to use a working rig to film the series: the noise is appalling.

After a while people start taking a vague interest in Kieran, and although they suspect he's a bit of a media tart, they begin talking to him.

Later, back in the relative warmth of Aberdeen, Kieran explains that the sense of isolation he felt as he began this project was the strongest yet of his career. The location didn't help; nor did his ignorance of the oil industry. But worse was the knowledge that he was embarking on something he didn't even know would come to fruition. 'At the beginning there is only the writer. Until you've started the script, there's nothing for anyone else to respond to; it's very isolating.'

Happily, that didn't last. The people on the Arctic rig thawed and, like the workers on the rigs he subsequently visited, soon realized that he wasn't there to dig dirt or write salacious scripts about sex-starved men leading accident-prone lives that were going to be nasty, brutish and short.

Initial resistance to outsiders is not a phenomenon exclusive to the oil industry, yet it, perhaps more than any other industry, has been traduced by both print and television journalists. Kieran found that the biggest problem prior to making the series was gaining the confidence of the people working offshore rather than the land-based chairmen and managers of oil companies. Later, as Moira discovered, the wariness of the latter would give way as soon as they realized what sort of series was being planned. And Kieran struck both gold and a friendship with one of the former: a man called Jonathan Cullen who, as he says, 'knows everything

Unloading supplies on the *Osprey Explorer*

Roughnecks

there is to know about oil rigs'. He became an invaluable source of material for the series – and an inspiration for one of the characters. 'He told me that, when he started working offshore, he was teased by his colleagues for knowing everything about everything – so they called him Ceefax.'

Yet Kieran himself was shortly to become something of a Ceefax about oil rigs – and that nearly became a problem. For a scriptwriter on this sort of series, it's important, yet difficult to prevent technical and factual details overwhelming the human drama of the piece. Talk to Kieran Prendiville and he'll tell you everything you ever wanted to know about oil rigs, but as he himself points out, 'Roughnecks' is not a documentary. 'It's a drama and the hardest part of writing drama is the structure. What are you going to do with all this research? There comes a point when you have to let go.' But not before you've gathered some vital information about the nature of the beast called 'oil rig'.

Initially, Kieran wasn't sure whether to set the series on an oil rig or on a production platform. The former are more specifically known as

The roughnecks

exploration or drilling rigs and do exactly what their name implies: they go exploring for oil or gas, drilling holes in the sea-bed and examining the cuttings brought up by the drill to establish whether or not there is an oil or gas field below.

If a very large field has been found, an oil rig will then be replaced by a production platform that will remain *in situ* for up to twenty years, their legs firmly driven into the sea bed, pumping the oil or gas out of the ground.

'It quickly became apparent,' says Kieran, 'that a drilling rig offered the best potential for the sort of drama the producers wanted. They're basic, pretty tiny, they generally sleep four to a cabin, there is only one recreation room, and there's nowhere to go and hide. Production platforms, on the other hand, can be like floating five-star hotels. They have gyms, lots of recreation rooms, the crew sleep only two to a cabin, sometimes they have televisions in the cabins, and the interior is carpeted.' Kieran's Arctic stint was on an exploration rig: he wasn't going to have a problem if he needed to infuse his characters with a sense of isolation and claustrophopia.

There were also practical and financial reasons why an exploration rig would be more suitable for a television series than a production platform. It is highly unlikely that an oil company would entertain the notion of allowing filming on a production platform: they are in constant use and it would be far too disruptive. It would also, as Kieran says, 'cost a trillion times as much to hire'.

Exploration rigs, on the other hand, are easily mobile and are not constantly in use. If there is a lull in the exploration industry, there will invariably be several rigs stacked in areas like the Cromarty Firth and the Firth of Forth. They are not defunct but remain on standby, manned by a skeleton crew, ready to be towed off to a potential drilling site at a moment's notice.

That's all very well, but supposing, when First Choice decide to go ahead with the project, the rig on which they are filming is called away? Ken Hodcroft, who at the end of the day organized the lease of a rig to First Choice for the second series of 'Roughnecks', says that very nearly *did* happen. 'It was touch and go for a moment. Just before we signed the contract it looked as if we were going to have to pull out of the deal. But once we'd signed it, there was no question of the rig moving. First Choice had exclusive use of it for the three weeks they were there. Anyway, what oil company would want to hire a rig with a bunch of actors on board?'

So, when it looked as if 'Roughnecks' was going to be a runner Kieran went off to develop the scripts, while Moira and Charles went shopping.

'We approached several oil companies,' says Moira, 'and they were all extremely co-operative and helpful, Shell in particular.' Echoing Kieran's words, she says that any initial resistance was due to the difficult time they'd had with previous series. 'They'd been burned in the past by accident-led series and were suspicious that we were going to make some sort of Piper Alpha disaster epic. But when they realized that 'Roughnecks' was going to be a sympathetic and honest portrayal of the rhythm of people's lives, they were very enthusiastic. They realized that it was going to do for the oil industry what 'The Bill' did for the police. And it helped that Kieran had written for 'The Bill'.'

Eventually, after viewing several rigs, they were offered the *Dan Countess*, a 'resting' yet fully operational rig owned by Aberdeen-based Lauritzen Offshore. Being twenty years old, it was fairly primitive by today's standards and therefore suitable for the sort of environment that the team had decided upon for 'Roughnecks'. Even better, it was based in the Cromarty Firth and not the Arctic. That meant it was a forty-minute helicopter flight from Aberdeen – a viable distance for the purposes of getting cast, crew and equipment there and back on a regular basis. The only problem was that, being on standby, it was too close to the shore. On

Director Sandy Johnson with actors Ricky Tomlinson and Annie Raitt

camera, the rig was supposed to look as if it was working. In reality, it was surrounded by other rigs and within sight of land. 'We had to tow it out to sea,' says Charles Elton, wincing at the memory. 'That cost us a fortune.'

But who exactly were they going to put on the rig, now re-named, for the purposes of the series, the *Osprey Explorer*? While the answer lay mainly with Kieran, everyone involved in pre-production worked closely in the development of the characters.

Moira and Charles were very keen to make a programme that was not star led. As Moira explains; 'We wanted the story to have as regional a feel as possible. One of the things that sustained my determination was a small scene in Ken Loach's "Riff Raff" where an actor I'd never seen before was sacked from a building site. That turned out to be Ricky Tomlinson who plays the chef in "Roughnecks".' This philosophy meant that Moira and Charles knew who they wanted for many of the characters before they reached the casting stage. According to Kieran, an important feature of 'Roughnecks' is the 'slice of life' aspect; the gradual revealing of the backgrounds and stories of a large and diverse cast of characters.

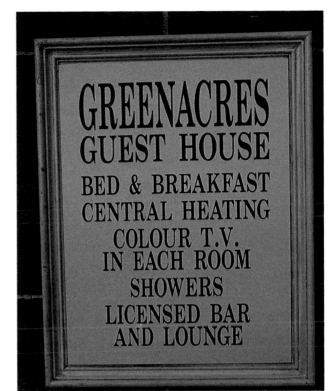

Greenacres, the fictional guest house where the roughnecks stayed during shore leave

'Given that we had now decided to call the series 'Roughnecks', I suppose I could have concentrated on the drilling floor itself,' says Kieran. 'After all, only the people on the drill floor itself are actually roughnecks.' Everybody else, he goes on to explain, has a different job title: from roustabout to oil installation manager (effectively, the captain); from cook to mud-logger. Strictly speaking, then, 'Roughnecks' is a misnomer as a title, 'But you have to use dramatic license somewhere.'

'The series,' continues Kieran, 'is driven by the roughnecks, but I didn't want to cut myself off from the others on the rig. And as the purpose is to see how everyone rubs along together, it would have defeated the object. These people are stuck together in a confined space for two weeks at a time. It's interesting to see what they do: what does the mechanic actually do? What does the cook actually cook? How do they relate to each other? I

Roughnecks

Preparing to film outside Greenacres

thought that would be far more interesting than just concentrating on the drill floor. Yes, I probably cheated a bit. As a rule, roughnecks don't hang around with the scientists and the catering staff generally stick together.'

Again research was vital to establish the accuracy of the characters' different roles. From stewards to chefs, derrickmen to crane-operators, tool-pushers to mechanics, Kieran talked to them all. Yet he had to tread a fine line in two ways: he had to make the scripts accurate and entertaining, and he had to give the characters a life onshore as well as offshore. 'Television viewers don't want to get bogged-down in the finer technicalities of the oil industry, but I had to make the whole thing realistic. And part of that realism involved copying the schedules of the rig crews. All of them work shifts of twelve hours on and twelve hours off for two weeks. Then they get two weeks' leave before repeating the process.'

There are, he goes on to explain, two crews working at any one time on the same rig, alternating their shifts in order to keep the rig working twenty four hours a day, three hundred and sixty five days a year. Oil rigs, like time and tide, wait for no man.

Charles Elton says that, from the point of view of the storylines, the division of time spent offshore and onshore was a big problem. 'We had to try to keep it right about who could be on duty, who was off duty, and who was onshore.' And both he and Kieran admit that they used a spot of artistic licence with their lives onshore.

'Most "real" rig crews I met,' says Kieran, 'lived in the big cities of Scotland or the Midlands; Glasgow, Manchester, Liverpool. And some – like "Cinders" the cook in the series – have other jobs to do. That,' Kieran points out, 'is indicative of the fact that the money offshore isn't as good as it used to be.'

The characters in 'Roughnecks,' however, seem to spend a lot of their time in Greenacres, the boarding house in Aberdeen run by Tom Butcher (the admin man and medic on the *Osprey Explorer*) and his wife Izzy. Does that mean they're social outcasts?

'No. It means they're characters in a television series and that it's logistically and financially impossible to follow them all onshore. 'Greenacres' was mainly a convenient mechanism for keeping the tension and holding all the characters together, but it is also based in reality. If your helicopter is going to leave for the rig at six in the morning, it makes sense to stay together – and close to the heliport.'

Kieran, however, spent a great deal of time close to the whisky bottle while he was doing his onshore research. His excuse – and he's sticking to it – is that by talking to rig crews in bars in Aberdeen, he got a real feel for the sort of characters who work offshore. In this research for character and situation he talked to endless people, drank buckets, spent a great deal of money (Aberdeen is not a cheap place to stay) and got extremely cold. 'Most of the time while I was in Aberdeen it was freezing. When I left, the taxi driver who took me to the airport said that when the sun shines it's a great city, that the sun made the granite sparkle and twinkle. He also said that when it rains the place is like a cemetery.'

Yet freezing cemetery or not, Aberdeen was greatly preferable to the Arctic Circle, and taught Kieran a lot about the people who work offshore. David Wilson, a colleague of Ken Hodcroft and the man who managed the actual rig used by First Choice in the second series, will testify to the accuracy of Kieran's characters. An ex-offshore worker himself, he knows what he's talking about. 'Oh yes, the characters in "Roughnecks" were absolutely true to life. You get some pretty weird and wonderful people offshore and the series really showed that.'

A tremendous accolade: but the point, as Kieran, Charles and Moira would argue, is that the characters are no more weird and wonderful than people in real life. There are those, like gentle giant Archie and lady-killing Chris, who are motivated by tangled or tragic love lives.

'Archie,' says Kieran, 'is one of those people you can find in any walk of life who refuses to believe that his relationship – in this case his marriage – is over. Even when it's staring him in the face; even when his wife remarries, he cannot accept the truth.'

Chris, on the other hand, is something of a lothario, but in need of the love of a good woman. The trouble is, he's not looking for a good woman ... Single and – as he's in charge of the drill floor with plenty of money, Chris has acquired a flat in Spain. Again, from his conversations in Aberdeen, Kieran discovered that a lot of offshore workers buy properties abroad. The trouble is, once they've set up their wives and families in such a lifestyle, they have to keep on working offshore to sustain it. And quite apart from the relatively good salary that a well-qualified rig worker can command, there are few other jobs in the world where you work two weeks on and two weeks off.

Then there are those who are slightly weary of life offshore – but can't – or haven't the motivation – to do anything else. Like Ian the mechanic, an ageing hippy who would much rather be walking in the mountains listening to the Incredible String Band and other sounds from the sixties.

Yet in direct contrast to Ian, there is Tessa the junior mechanic, who has been positively itching to work offshore and jumps at the opportunity to do so. But *do* a lot of women work offshore?

'Oh yes,' says Kieran, neatly debunking the myth of an exclusively male environment. 'There are plenty of women offshore, but mainly on production platforms rather than rigs.' With reference to Tessa and her colleague Hilary, he adds that 'I was told there weren't any women mechanics or mud-loggers on rigs so I thought, "well, soon there *will* be"; let's start with my fictional ones.' Kieran's informer, however, turned out to be ill-informed. His story of the dearth of women was published in the *Sunday Times* and Kieran later received an indignant letter from a reader. 'I am a woman mechanic in the North Sea,' it read, 'and all my best friends are woman mechanics.'

Francesca Hunt, who was to play the part of Hilary, liked the fact that her character was slightly aloof and, when filming began, played down Hilary's femininity. 'Hilary wasn't remotely girlie: none of us thought that would be appropriate anyway.'

Hywel Simons training in the pool at the RGIT

Later, however, Francesca was more than a little nonplussed when, in an Aberdeen hotel, she saw a petite, smartly-dressed and very feminine girl surrounded by a whole bunch of hard-drinking hairy riggers. 'I got into conversation with her and discovered that she was the driller! Not only that, but she had started life offshore as a roughneck and worked her way up. I was slightly taken aback and thought, 'Oh God, have I got Hilary wrong?' But then Francesca goes on to add that the female driller – frilly blouse notwithstanding – gave as good as she got to her male colleagues: exactly as Hilary does.

But what about the character who took more flak from his workmates than anyone else: Wilf, or 'Village'; the initially cocky young

Welshman who gets several sharp shocks on his first stint offshore? (He was also given his nickname; by Chris who, after hearing where he came from, uttered the immortal line 'So what do they do for an idiot when you're away from home?'.)

In the life raft
at the RGIT

Kieran laughs at the mention of the hapless Welshman. 'Yeah – poor old Village was a bit of a throwback really. He arrives in Aberdeen in a stetson and check shirt and *nobody* has looked like that in Aberdeen since at least 1972.'

Village has a completely idealized vision of what life offshore is like – and part of his näivety comes out in the scene where he tries to smuggle vodka offshore by injecting it into oranges. Many rig crews will testify that the vodka-in-orange trick is part of offshore mythology and, for Kieran, it was a wonderful and authentic way to illustrate the fact that alcohol is strictly forbidden offshore. 'I believe that you are allowed a couple of cans a day or something in the Norwegian sector – but everywhere else you'll get bumped if you have even the slightest whiff of alcohol on your breath.'

And the reason for the total ban on alcohol? 'There are already twenty ways to kill yourself on an oilrig. You don't need any more.'

Roughnecks

Focus puller Mary Kyte dressed to face the elements

The dangers of life offshore combined with the claustrophobic atmosphere of a rig lead, paradoxically, to a constant and sometimes relentless light-heartedness. As Alec Westwood, who plays roughneck Davey Rains, points out, 'you've got to keep the atmosphere light and jokey because if anything gets heavy it's ten times more intense than on land because of the claustrophobia. Any little thing gets well out of hand.' And Alec should know. Not only does his character get out of hand at one point, but Alec himself has personal experience of oil rigs: he used to work on one.

Most of the practical jokes are played on the newcomers. The joy of the one played on 'Village', – telling him to set out the chairs on the helideck for Sunday Service – is that it could so easily have happened in real life. If, like 'Village', you're a rookie roustabout (basically a dogsbody) you're regarded as fair game for the cruellest jokes. In real life, roustabouts have been sent out at night to the north side of the rig on 'iceberg watch', armed with a 'berg-pole' to fight off the offending mountains of ice. Other stories include roustabouts being charged for their food and laundry (everything on a rig comes free). The food in rigs is generally of the five-star variety and one newcomer's colleagues saw fit to charge him accordingly. He finished his two-week stint broke and in debt.

Cruel these jokes may be, but everyone insists they're not played out of malice or personal dislike. It's all part of the process of becoming 'one of the lads' – regardless of what sex you are. In that respect, being part of a rig crew is not dissimilar to being part of a theatre company or a film unit: you have no choice but to learn to rub along together. And that, of course, is exactly what Moira Williams wanted to portray in 'Roughnecks'.

Kieran, while soaking up the atmosphere in Aberdeen and developing ideas for characters and storylines, found himself constantly battling to fit his factual research round his fictional drama. Aware that television audiences have no wish to be bombarded with more technical jargon than they need, Kieran had to bear in mind that the premise of the series is what life is like on a rig – not what it *might* be like. And that also meant he had to bear in mind the type of rig they were using. For the viewer with no knowledge of rigs, that might seem unimportant, but those in the know would be able to spot that the story was based on a semi-submersible and not a jack-up rig. While both types are exploration rigs, the latter has legs that rest on the sea bed while the former floats on legs buoyed up by giant caissons some sixty feet under the surface of the water. (Anchors going down into the sea bed keep the rig from drifting). The limitation of jack-up rigs is their inability to drill in deep water – and in the middle of the North Sea the water is extremely deep. Kieran, therefore, knew he had to use a semi-submersible in 'Roughnecks'.

'I laid various clues,' he explains, 'about the things that could go wrong on a semi-submersible; culminating in the crash in episode six.'

But if the series isn't 'accident-led', isn't having a helicopter crash a bit on the sensational side?

Kieran disagrees and, it turns out, with reason. The biggest fear of every oilman and woman, it seems, is the journey to work. No matter how many times they've flown offshore in a helicopter, they dread the experience each time. And the accident statistics bear out their fears. Every fifteen months

Filming outside Morag's house

or so a helicopter ditches in the North Sea, and while this doesn't necessarily result in fatalities or even injuries, it is a desperate and frightening experience.

Helicopter crashes contributed to the formation of an organization called the Offshore Women's Link Support, or OWLS; a support group for the partners of men who work on rigs. Hazel Kemp is a member and is only too aware of the dangers of helicopters flying out to rigs in the sometimes appalling weather in the North Sea. 'There's the anxiety you always face,' she says, 'of worrying whenever you hear a helicopter overhead. Ever since the Chinook, Brent Spar and Cormorant disasters (where helicopters crashed), I've hated that sound.'

'There can be few scarier things,' adds Kieran, 'than flying in a chopper over the North Sea in a force-ten hurricane and hearing the skipper say "ditching, ditching, ditching".'

Because of the dangers inherent in this particular mode of travelling to work, everyone who goes offshore is required to undergo the Survival Course at RGIT (Robert Gordon's Institute of Technology) in Aberdeen. Kieran, by coincidence, had already done the course ten years previously when researching a programme for 'Tomorrow's World'. Even so, he was required to take a refresher course. Later, all the cast and crew of 'Roughnecks' took the course as well. This was partly because some of them would have to act the part in the helicopter-crash episode: but it was mainly because they might find themselves doing it for real. Whoever said acting was a cushy job?

It was over lunch that Moira Williams and Charles Elton popped the question to director Sandy Johnson. 'Oh, yes,' remembers Sandy, 'we had a great time and a fairly liquid lunch and (this was nothing to do with the effect of the liquid) I had no hesitation in coming on board as the director of 'Roughnecks'. It felt close to home.'

Home, for Sandy, is now London but he hails from near Loch Lomond. And by a greater coincidence, his mother was living close to where they were filming 'Roughnecks'.

'I tried to get a helicopter to fly over my mother's house,' he recalls, 'but on the only day I could do it Clint Eastwood had booked the helicopter to go off for a round of golf at Gleneagles.'

Now that's what we like: Hollywood types flying about being glamorous. And then Sandy, like Kieran before him and everyone else after him, spoils it all. 'No, it's not glamorous. It's dangerous.' Sandy goes on to illustrate that point in vivid colours. Because the shooting schedule they had drawn

Opposite: Director Sandy Johnson

The cast leaving the helicopter

up required them to film the oil-rig interiors at Bray Studios, Sandy was keen to have an early examination of the *Dan Countess/Osprey Explorer* so that those interiors would be realistic. To that end, he and several of the crew flew out to the rig long before shooting began. 'The first time we flew out it was in a black helicopter. Two weeks later, we went out again, with the same pilot but in a white helicopter. I asked him in a conversational sort of way what had happened to the black one: he replied that he'd crashed it into some electricity pylons. It was, apparently, the third time he'd crashed.'

'Oh yes, we continued to use him. We got some great shots when we were flying with him at about a hundred miles an hour one foot above the waves.'

Sandy must be made of pretty stern stuff. 'I was screaming,' he adds.

Sandy's experience as a director, encompassing both television and film, has taken him all over the world. His television films include 'The Comic Strip Presents,' 'Dirty Movie' and 'Slags', and he has directed episodes of 'Inspector Morse', 'The Ruth Rendell Mysteries', 'Gone To The Dogs' and its follow-up 'Gone To Seed'. Film-wise, he has just completed a feature set in Liverpool and the States and is about to embark on an adaptation of Glasgow writer Alistair Grey's *Poor Things*. How, then, does filming on an oil-rig compare to everything else? One would imagine that it would be difficult, cramped and dangerous.

'You've got to remember,' says Sandy, 'that the whole way of life on a rig is based on moving heavy stuff around by crane and on flying things on and off on a regular basis. That makes it a positive advantage for a film crew. What's more, it was actually a joy to work in such an enclosed world; the limitations of the environment create the parameters within which you work. Certain movies work on that level as well – prison movies, desert island ones – you already have a stage to work on.'

Sandy goes on to say that, if anything, filming *off* the rig was more complicated: the real world comes into the frame. And from a practical point of view, shooting on the rig was a joy. 'We could, for instance, put a camera in a bucket on the end of a crane and get some terrific wide shots of the rig.'

For Sandy, as for everyone else, the big problem was one of time. The shooting schedule – and indeed Lauritzen Offshore's rental of the rig to First Choice – allowed for three weeks shooting time on the rig itself. Not much for a seven-hour series where most of the action happens on the rig. Yet, with all the interior shots being done in the studio, it meant that only the external shots had to be done offshore. It still wasn't easy.

But before anything happened, they had to get the entire cast, and production crew including cameramen, lighting technicians, engineers, wardrobe and make-up out to the rig.

Chapter two

Back row, left to right:
Charles Elton, Producer;
Sue Quinn, Location
Manager; Clive Russell;
Julian Ashby, Design
Assistant; Moira
Williams, Producer;
Brian Binns, Second
Assistant Director;
Francesca Hunt; Sandy
Johnson, Director; Jo
Rickard, Wardrobe
Assistant; Paul Copley.
Front row, left to right:
Verity Hawkes,
Wardrobe Supervisor;
George Rossi; Alec
Westwood; Hywel
Simons; Francesco Reidy,
First Assistant Director;
Barney Reisz, Associate
Producer.

27

▲

Discovery

▼

There is a photograph of the cast and crew of 'Roughnecks' just before they flew off to the *Dan Countess* for the first six days of shooting. They are all grinning broadly. 'It's a fraud,' says Moira. 'The smiles were all forced. Most of us were terrified of getting into that helicopter.' Despite the fact that they had done the rigorous RGIT Survival Course, this was to be the first helicopter ride for many of them.

'The point was,' continues Moira, 'it was a *long* ride – and right over the North Sea. And the survival course had served to emphasize the very

Filming at the heliport

real dangers of what we were doing: we had been trained to deal with an accident; trained on how to react if the helicopter were to ditch in the North Sea.'

Francesca Hunt says the course made her feel a lot safer. 'It made me realize just how useless I would have been in a disaster.'

'No matter how many times rig crews have flown out to rigs,' says Kieran to emphasize the point, 'they have to watch a safety video prior to each journey. And if they're seen not to be paying attention – they can be bumped. It's no joke.'

Freya Pinsent, the production accountant on 'Roughnecks', is now an expert on helicopters, 'But no – I didn't fly in one. Terrified.' She is, however, quick to point out that Bristows, the helicopter company used by the 'Roughnecks' team, were extraordinarily helpful

Terry played by Bruce Jones with Teresa Banham who plays Tessa

and have an impressive safety record. 'They were extremely kind and let us use their heliport as one of our locations.'

Freya's job, once the budget for the series had been agreed, was to make sure they kept to that budget. An alarming task, one would think.

'Well,' says Freya, 'there were two costs that you don't normally encounter in television series. One was the actual oil rig itself. We were effectively renting both the rig and the crew from Lauritzen and paid for all 'on-board' expenses. Additionally – and this *was* expensive – we had to tow the rig further out to sea.'

The other expense was the hire of the helicopters. 'The big ones – Super Pumas or S-61s – appear in a lot of the shots and we used at weekends to get everyone off the rig. The little ones – S-76s – we used every day to collect the rushes, bring in supplies, and ferry in the odd actor.' Furthermore, they sometimes used both helicopters simultaneously to film air-to-air shots – and none of that comes cheap.

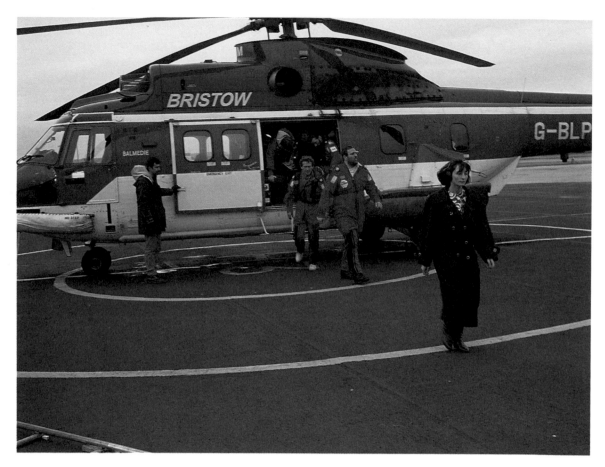

'If anything had gone wrong,' continues Freya, 'we could have been in real trouble. The weather, for instance; you can't insure against bad weather and we were very lucky with that. Almost too lucky.'

Moira agrees. 'The night before we were all due to go out to the rig to begin filming, the weather forecast was appalling. We had been warned to expect storms and hurricanes and all the other things you get in the North Sea in November. Most of the sea was, in fact, engulfed by storms, but we were somehow in a little oasis of sunshine.' All very good and well but as Moira goes on to explain, it looked as if they were in the Bahamas.

'When I saw the rushes of the first few days' filming I was horrified: nothing but endless blue skies.' Luckily, the weather broke after the second week and everyone got drenched, buffeted by hurricanes and nearly froze to death. It begs the question: how did everyone cope?

Cast and crew alike laugh at the memory of their arrival on the rig. The 'real' rig crew were, to say the least, sceptical. For the purposes of verisimilitude, First Choice had reached an agreement with Lauritzen

Rigging a helicopter with a camera for an aerial shot

Offshore that they would hire members of the real crew – in addition to the skeleton crew – to make the rig look as if it was in operation. Furthermore, the real crew were to act as instructors for the various parts the actors were playing: mechanics, crane-operators, tool-pushers and so on. None of them had previously worked with actors and were more than a little doubtful – not to say amused – at the prospect. As Moira so succinctly puts it, 'who wants a bunch of luvvies descending on your rig?' And Liam Cunningham, playing driller Chris Cassidy, was later told that some of them thought they were going to be invaded by 'Merchant Ivory types'. Heaven help the white linen.

The consensus, then, was that the oilmen on the *Dan Countess* reckoned the 'Roughnecks' team wouldn't last a minute. One can't blame them. Actors – undeservedly – have a reputation for being precious, for acting like prima donnas. They are supposed to be demanding; they want limos and trailers and they don't want to get their hair wet. It's not surprising that the crew of the *Dan Countess* were more than a little dubious about the descending luvvies.

David Wilson, who worked on the second series, remembers: 'my main concern was safety. There's great potential for getting hurt on a rig – a potential exacerbated by all the cameras and cables they brought with them – and my problem was that I didn't know what these people would actually be *doing*. If you like, I was there to educate them. I wouldn't let them do anything,' he adds, 'until they'd had a safety briefing and until we'd finished shifting all the containers housing their equipment. It would have been only too easy for someone to get crushed between them. There isn't,' he adds, 'very much room on a rig.'

So how did the actors react to being offshore? David Wilson – not entirely convincingly – replies that they seemed to enjoy it. 'But I think they felt a bit restricted: no alcohol or night-clubbing.'

So: what exactly is it like being on a rig? How did they enjoy it?

'Oil Rigs are horrible places. How would you like to live on the set of 'Alien' for three weeks?'

Liam Cunningham

Oh come on, Liam; it can't be that bad.

'It's worse. An oil rig is basically an overgrown Black & Decker drill with up to sixty people working on it.'

Ah. Leaving Liam for a moment and pressing on to the analogy he

Roughnecks

Filming on the rig

made, you find that it's actually a very accurate one. People do not go onto oil rigs for fun: they go to work. And the hub of the work activity happens on the drill floor.

That floor is noisy, smelly, cold, usually wet and always dangerous. It's where the roughnecks work for twelve hours at a stretch, with only the occasional break in the smoke-filled coffee shack. Colum Convey, who plays the roughneck Ceefax, admits that, while they were all told exactly what roughnecks do, they only experienced enough of the job to realize that acting is, by comparison, a cushy number.

Roughnecks are the crucial manning force on the floor. Their job is to work as a team, in conjunction with the derrickman from aloft – and under the guidance of the driller – to drill for oil. This involves connecting the drill bit (effectively, the bit that actually makes the hole) to a string of hollow steel pipes at the rotary table in the centre of the drill floor. Then they raise the pipe sections by block and tackle system; they lift and place wedges to support the weight of the drill string (a section of three pipes is called a string) when adding new sections of pipe. They also unscrew the pipes with large mechanical tongs and then constantly repeat the whole process as drill bits become worn and the whole system withdrawn and replaced.

To give some idea of just what an onerous task this is, it helps to realize the length-to-diameter ratio of the pipe that twists the drill bit: it is about the same as if a dentist was operating his own drill with his patient at the far end of a football pitch. The sea bed may be ten thousand feet below: the hole drilled is generally a little less than nine inches in diameter. Hence the derrick, the pointy bit that looks like the Eiffel Tower.

Over fifty metres high, the derrick is used to stack the pipes when they are being withdrawn so that a new drill bit can be connected. To do this, the derrickman climbs to the monkey board high in the derrick and guides the pipes into position. Pipes that have not yet been used are kept in the pipe rack and are lifted in bundles by crane onto a catwalk. Then they are measured before being winched, one by one, to the drill floor.

So the noise is constant; the machinery enormous; there are metal catwalks and stairways everywhere – and it is an extremely dangerous environment. All you need is Sigourney Weaver charging about in her underpants and you really do have a duplicate of the set of 'Alien.'

Bruce Jones being instructed in the delicate art of running an oil rig

Roughnecks

The crane on the *Osprey Explorer*

And in terms of size, rigs are deceptive structures. Although, as Charles Elton says, 'they look tiny when you fly in from the air but appear to be great hulking masses of metal when you're on them,' much of this mass isn't useable. Some of it is metal gangways and staircases, and a lot of it is reserved for specific, potentially dangerous storage or, as with the control room, operational purposes. There is actually very little room to walk around. Add the cables and lights and the forty or so extra people, and one has some idea of the potential hazards.

All very well, but the 'Roughnecks' people were acting – not working the rig. In the event that made very little difference as to the sort of life they led aboard the *Dan Countess*. Because of the tight schedule, they had to film at least twelve hours a day – and in all weathers. And because of the dangers, they had to wear hard hats and protective clothing at all times.

'People are hugely danger conscious,' says Moira Williams. 'Everywhere is an oily zone or a wet zone or a danger zone – except the womb-like interior – which is incredibly cramped. All dirty outdoor clothes and footwear have to be taken off before you go inside. But woe betide any of us who tried to go out without a hard hat – we'd get yelled at.'

MUD, GLORIOUS MUD

'Without mud there would be no oil.' So says Kieran Prendiville – and he's right. Drilling mud is the lifeblood of the oil industry, and the job of a mud-logger or mud engineer is one of the most interesting, complex and responsible on a rig.

But first the mud itself. It isn't mud as we know it, but a viscous substance made of chemicals (including the sulphate barite, which lends it its muddy appearance) mixed with oil and water. It performs several vital functions in the drilling process. Pumped down through the drill pipe and then up between the outside of the pipe and the walls of the bore hole, it lubricates the bearings and cools the drill bit as it cuts into the rock. Additionally, it becomes plastered against the sides of the hole to reduce the chance of a cave-in and – should a pocket of high-pressure gas be encountered – it is heavy enough to hold the gas back and stop it blowing up the well. In that respect, the weight and viscosity of the drilling mud is critical.

Lastly, drilling mud comes back up the drilling pipe, bringing with it the vital fragments of rock cuttings that will be analysed by the mud-logger. These fragments indicate, by their fossil content, the type and age of the rock being drilled and reveal the presence of oil or gas. The mud logger, therefore, is the lynchpin of the exploration: the one who will discover if the oil company leasing the rig is wasting its time or sitting, effectively, on a gold-mine.

The popular idea that the oil itself is stored in a vast underground tank which can be easily drained is, unfortunately a misconception. The oil is housed in solid – albeit porous – rock, and does not give up its liquid easily. Fears that the seabed could collapse are, then, unfounded: even when the oil is removed, its place is taken by gas or water.

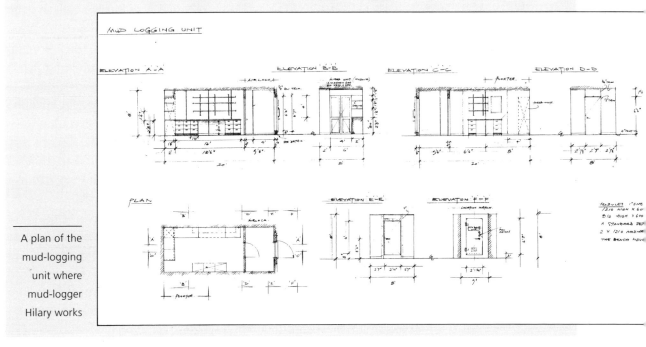

A plan of the mud-logging unit where mud-logger Hilary works

Roughnecks

One of the costume team dirtying Village's clean overalls in preperation for the shoot

The visitors also had to abide by the no-alcohol rule; they had to sleep four to a cabin ('four to a wardrobe', as Liam Cunningham puts it) – and they developed the rig crew's disease of being isolated on a lump of metal in the middle of the sea while at the same time suffering from claustrophobia.

Yet the interesting thing about their reactions is that they all vary: some of them hated the rig, a lot of them loved it but admitted they couldn't live on it for ever; all of them declared that it was a fantastic experience and one that they wouldn't have missed for anything. More revealing, they all became tremendously chummy with the 'real' crew. That, for Moira Williams, was an enormous relief.

'At first the people on the rig were *very* cagey,' she says. 'They were perfectly courteous but of course they were just as apprehensive as we were. But by the end of the first night everyone was covered in oil and had begun to laugh together and by the end of the second night everyone had exchanged news and photos of families and the men had started reading our scripts and giving pointers. It was one of the greatest moments of the whole shoot,' adds Moira with feeling, 'when I realized we were all going to get·on. We all started to play games in the evening: Trivial Pursuit, Monopoly, poker – you name it, we did it. It was terrific fun. The men on the rig joined in. In fact, they were absolutely fantastic in every way – and Ricky Tomlinson, who plays Cinders, turned out to be a brilliant quiz master.'

'The interplay,' says Charles Elton, 'between 'us and them' was fascinating to watch. At first, as Moira says, there was wariness on both sides. But after a while, it became impossible to tell us apart – particularly as everyone was wearing the same clothes.'

'It was hysterical,' says Sandy Johnson. 'The rig crew were just magic – so funny. What I suppose we all realized was that we *had* to survive. In that respect we were no different from real offshore workers. The fact that there

'Roughnecks' producers Charles Elton and Moira Williams

is no alcohol allowed,' he muses, 'is actually very interesting. It means that everyone has to turn to other things for amusement. It was amazing going into the recreation room; you'd see groups of people huddled together playing Monopoly, and cards – and the quiz night in episode two is exactly like the quiz nights we ourselves had.'

The lack of alcohol was something of a problem. 'Actually, it was a bit of a killer for all of us,' admits Moira. 'That's what film crews do, you see – they drink! It was a bit of a revelation to wind down after a twelve-hour day with a cup of cocoa ...'

'It was the first time in living memory,' laughs Charles, 'that a British film crew has been up at 6am fresh as a daisy. On location there are usually people still propping up the bar at three in the morning. As a sort of compensation, when we were staying at the Holiday Inn in Aberdeen, we did a deal with the management that the bar should remain open until the last person left. One day,' he adds in awe (and perhaps regret) 'there was still someone in the bar at eight in the morning ...'

Liam Cunningham is the first to admit that, despite his dislike of oil rigs, the atmosphere was tremendous. 'Although I retch at the thought of another game of Scrabble, I must say the whole experience was the best of my career so far. I've never been with *less* egocentric people in my life. An oil rig may be the most boring place under the sun, but the people we were with – all of them – were fantastic.'

David Wilson, with his personal experience of working offshore, is the first to agree about the boredom factor. When asked about the accuracy of the portrayal of life offshore, he replies that 'they dramatized everything too much. Life on a rig is actually extremely boring – but then they had to overdramatize, didn't they? Nobody would watch the series otherwise. But they got the technical details right. They were always asking us about those. And they also got the characters right. What's more, they were really friendly; a really nice bunch of people. Initially our guys thought they'd be a bunch of stuck-up film stars – but we were all wrong. Mind you,' he muses, 'it must have been tough going for them with all that standing about and waiting to act. At least our guys work all the time.'

But all actors are used to standing about waiting to act – if not always in a force-twelve hurricane. Everyone agrees that, after the Indian Summer of the first two weeks, the dramatic change in weather took them by surprise. Francesca Hunt (Hilary), laughs when she remembers it. 'It served us right, really. The men on the rig had been saying 'just you wait' and of course we'd replied that we *couldn't* wait; that we were positively dying to experience the North Sea at its worst. Well ... we got our come-

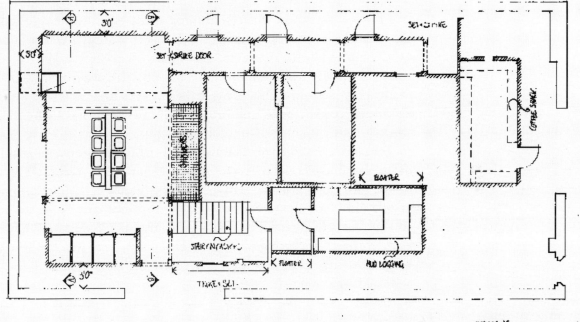

ROUGHNECKS II — STAGE III BRAY STUDIO'S — RIG INTERIOR — SCALE ¼"

A plan of the small stage at Bray where parts of the rig set, including the coffee shack, were built

uppance, didn't we?' Francesca goes on to explain that, when they found themselves in a force-twelve hurricane, she went to look at the 'spirit-level sort of thing' in the control room. 'On a scale of plus to minus five, it measures the sway of the rig, and up till then it had been hovering around the zero mark. During the hurricane, it veered all the way to both fives ...'

Bruce Jones, who plays Terry the offshore installation manager (O.I.M.), recalls trying to get up to a catwalk to film a scene during the hurricane. 'I made absolutely no progress climbing that metal staircase on the outside of the rig. At one point the only thing going upwards was the rain!'

But what did they do when they weren't acting? Playing games, no matter how amusing, has its limitations. There is nowhere to exercise – unless you feel like doing several thousand laps of the heli-pad. Cable and satellite television is a possibility, but then the television is in the rec room which is full of smoke and people playing games ...

One of the activities enjoyed by members of the cast and crew (and in which you cannot indulge on a working rig) was fishing. They formed the 'Cod Club' and fished over the side every night. Nobody caught a thing – unless you count the whale. 'I went rushing into the rec room one night,' recalls Alec Westwood, one of the failed fishermen, 'shouting at everyone that there was a minke whale swimming about beneath the rig. They all came out to look: it was a magical sight; this enormous creature beneath us, illuminated by the rig lights.' The whale – accompanied by its baby – came back every night: not because it found the occupants of the rig particularly interesting, but because that was the time when the kitchens ejected all the left-over food into the sea. Perhaps that's why nobody caught a fish.

As Colum Convey says, 'What fish in its right mind would go anywhere near a pathetic piece of bait when they can have fillet steak?' So it's just as well they didn't need to catch fish to survive. Anyway, sometimes other people did it for them. Sandy Johnson recalls that one of the most delightful and unexpected treats was, one morning, a visit from a fishing boat. 'We lowered a bucket down to them and they filled it to the brim with langoustines they had just caught. We gave the langoustines to the chef and had them for lunch. Fantastic!'

Yet anyone familiar with rigs will know that fantastic food is not unusual. The catering on North-Sea rigs is renowned for being of an exceptionally high standard – and the *Dan Countess* was no exception. Everyone – cast and crew alike – ate extremely well and, because they weren't working at the same punishing speed as a rig crew, they put on weight – an obvious problem from a continuity and practical point of view. Shortly after they arrived, several actors were measured for dry suits which would be used later in the shoot. In the event, they were never needed and thus never made. Just as well: the actors all expanded by half an inch while they were offshore.

So given the standard of the food, and the fact that many of the chefs have worked in five-star hotels, wasn't it a bit cruel to make the cook on 'Roughnecks' such a disaster? 'Yes,' says Kieran Prendiville. 'It was really rotten to chefs in the North Sea. Let's call it a bit of artistic licence.'

It's just as well it was only artistic licence and not real life: Ricky Tomlinson who plays 'Cinders' the cook, freely admits he can't even boil water. Yet in spite of the privations of life offshore, everyone who stayed on the *Dan Countess* remembers it as one of the most enjoyable experiences of their career. Even those who wouldn't work on a rig 'no

Cinders with the rig's
real catering staff

matter how much they payed me' insist that the camaraderie between everyone was extraordinary – and extraordinarily unusual.

When pressed to spill some dirt and asked to drop the 'Darling it was wonderful' stance, everyone has a response along the lines of 'I *know* it sounds precious and actory, but it's *true*!' It must, then, be true: and it speaks volumes for everyone on the rig – cast, crew and rig-crew alike – that the atmosphere was so congenial. It could have been a disaster. Instead it was a roaring success.

But what of the actual technicalities of filming?

Roughnecks

9. At the second set of lights continue straight over into EAST NORTH STREET, HARBOUR A956, DUNDEE, PERTH A92.

10. At the next roundabout take the 3RD TURNING signposted INNER RING ROAD, DUNDEE, PERTH, and HARBOUR.

11. At the next set of lights turn right into VIRGINIA STREET, signposted to DUNDEE and PERTH A956.

12. Follow the road past the NCP car park and onto the TRINITY QUAYSIDE.

13. At the mini roundabout turn all the way round and go back up TRINITY QUAY.

14. Take your first left by the New Swan Bar and the sign Aberdeen Maritime Museum, into SHIP ROW.

15. Follow the road to the right into the one way system.

16. Await location instructions for parking.
    - CANON cinema car park
    - On the back of NCP car park courtyard

MOVEMENT ORDER 16 CONTINUED

FROM: UNIT BASE
TO: THE PAINT SHOP
    THE GREEN
    ABERDEEN

...ET RUNNING FROM REGENTS QUAY TO

...d turn left.
...o Market Street
...den street.
...he road through to the green.
...shop on the right hand side.
...t into the NCP carpark opposite
...tions

...ACK TO UNIT BASE.
...arpark and drive back to Market
...and turn immediately left at the
...the New Swan Bar and the sign
...nto SHIP ROW.
...t into the one way system.
...back of the NCP carpark on the

Running orders for 'Roughnecks' and blueprints for the interior of Greenacres

ROUGHNECKS

PRODUCERS: CHARLES ELTON, MOIRA WILLIAMS, SANDY JOHNSON		SUNRISE. 06:45			
DIRECTOR: BARNEY REISZ		SUNSET. 17:15			

CALLSHEET NO 37
DATE WED 3/11/93

ASSOCIATE PRODUCER: 0831 829221
LOCATION
PAINT SHOP THE GREEN,ABERDEEN MARKET
PUB TILTED WIG,UNION STREET
NIGHT CLUB AS ABOVE

ADDRESS

MAIN UNIT: 11:00
COSTUME: 10:45
MAKE UP: 09:45

CONTACTS
1ST AD 0831 392563
2ND AD 0831 141174

EP/SC	INT/EXT	NO OF PAGES	D/N	STORY LOCATION	CHARACTERS	ARTISTES
2/34A	EXT	2/8	D 6	PAINT SHOP	MORAG	JULIET CADZOW
MORAG NARROWLY AVOIDS A TRUCK				VILLAGE		HYWEL SIMONS
1/8	EXT	1/8	D 1	PUB		HYWEL SIMONS
ESTABLISHER.					VILLAGE	KEITH HUTCHEON
1/9	INT	2 1/8	D 1	PUB	BARMAN	JOANNAE BETT
					JACKIE	VICKY MASSON
					PAULINE	
VILLAGE GETS COLD SHOULDER FROM JACKIE AND PAULINE.						
4/65	EXT	1/8	N 16	NIGHT CLUB	ESTABLISHER	LIAM CUNNINGHAM
					CHRIS	ASHLEY JENSEN
4/67	EXT	4/8	N 16	BAR	HEATHER	
CHRIS AND HEATHER DECIDE TO WALK.						

ARTIST	CHARACTER	P/UP	M/UP	W/D	ON SET
JULIET CADZOW	MORAG	09:15	09:45	10:45	11:00
HYWEL SIMONS	VILLAGE	11:45	13:15	12:15	13:30
KEITH HUTCHEON	BARMAN	O.T.	AS REQ	12:15	AS REQ
JOANNE BETT	JACKIE	10:00	11:00	13:15	AS REQ
VICKY MASSON	PAULINE	O.T.	11:45	13:15	AS REQ
LIAM CUNNINGHAM	CHRIS	17:00	17:30	18:45	AS REQ
ASHLEY JENSEN	HEATHER	17:00	18:00	17:45	AS REQ

SUPPORTING ARTISTS	DESCRIPTION	P/UP	M/UP	W/D	ON SET
2/34A	(PASSERS)	O.T.	AS REQ	AS REQ	11:00
1/9 SEE AD'S LIST	20 X SMART PUNTERS STAFF				
	(FROM 1/9)				
1/8	(PASSERS) BOUNCER	O.T.	AS REQ	18:45	AS REQ
4/65 PATRICK BRAND	(PASSERS)				
4/67					

DOWN

BAR

TRANSPORT MINIBUS C/O TINA HENRY 0224 586586/0651 872580

UNIT TRANSPORT - ALL THOSE "NOT" TRAVELLING IN DEDICATED VEHICLES

10:30 HRS PROMPT MINIBUS TO DEPART FROM HOTEL RECEPTION - TO ARRIVE
AT 11:00 HRS .NB TO INCLUDE JENNY BOOST.

CAST/COSTUME/MAKE-UP

MINIBUS TO DEPART 09:15 HRS AND TO INCLUDE:
BRIAN, AMANDA, DAWN, JULIET CADZOW, NORMA

FRANCESCO ROVER 414

TO COLLECT SANDY AND JOHN DALY AND DEPART HOLIDAY INN RECEPTION
10:30 HRS

TILLIE WILLIAMS - ROVER 414

0:00 PICK UP HOWARD, VERITY, JO, AND JOANNE BETT FROM HOTEL RECEPTION
AND PROCEED TO UNIT BASE.

11:45 PICK UP HYWEL SIMONS FROM THE HOTEL RECEPTION
UNIT BASE.

17:00 PICK UP LIAM CUN...
RECEPTION AND PROCEED TO...

ACTION VEHICLES

6 X TAXIS AS PER MIKE SM...
TRUCK AS PER BILL (PROPS...

CATERING

LUNCH TO BE AVAILABLE FR...
DINNER AT 19:00 HRS FOR...

ELECTRICAL/GENNY AS PER...
1 X CHERRY PICKER - PL...
EXTRA GENNY.

FACILITIES

ALL FACILITIES TO BE UP...

PRODUCTION/LOCATION NOTE...

ANYONE WISHING TO BRING...
PRODUCTION AND THEN WITH...

RUSHES PICK UP 17:30 HRS...

ADVANCE SCHEDULE 4/11/9...
TAXI/MONTAGE/BAR/DOCKS...
4/61 7/76 6/8(1) 6/8(2)...
4/68 6/1

'ROUGHNECKS' PRODUCTION OFFICE:
C/O Holiday Inn Crowne Plaza
Old Meldrum Road
Bucksburn AB2 9LN
Tel. 0224-713-911
Fax. 0224-714-020

2.11.93

'ROUGHNECKS' MOVEMENT ORDER NO. 16

DATE: WEDNESDAY 3RD NOVEMBER 1993

LOCATION 1: PAINT SHOP
ADDRESS: TOP FASHIONS
            64 THE GREEN   DISTANCE: 5 MILES
            ABERDEEN   TIME: 20 MINUTES
                                    TRUCKS: 30 MINUTES
CONTACT: MRS PANG

LOCATION 2: TILTED WIG PUB
ADDRESS: 55 CASTLE STREET   TEL: 0224 211890
            ABERDEEN

CONTACT: Maureen McMann

HOSPITAL: Forest Hill Hospital A & E Unit

                                    TEL: 0224
POLICE: Queen Street, Aberdeen   TEL: 0224 681818

TOILETS: Inside the locations   TEL: 0224 639111
         Portaloos by the UNIT BASE in Shiprow.

UNIT BASE: BEHIND THE NCP CARPARK, SHIPROW.

1. Turn right out of the hotel MAIN ENTRANCE into MALCOLM ROAD
    and turn immediately right again into OLD MELDRUM ROAD
    towards the main road.

2. At the traffic lights turn left into the INVERURIE ROAD/
    AUCHMILL ROAD A96, and head towards ABERDEEN.

3. Keep following the signs for THE CITY CENTRE A96 over the
    next roundabout and the next 4 sets of lights.

4. At the next junction with the A978 to FRASERBURGH, continue
    straight on on the A96 TOWARDS THE CITY CENTER.

5. At the next set of lights continue straight over into POWIS
    TERRACE.

6. Follow the road to the left at the signpost for CITY CENTER
    EAST, HARBOUR.

7. At the next roundabout take the second left signposted INNER
    RING ROAD, DUNDEE A96, PERTH A956 AND HARBOUR into WEST
    NORTH STREET.

8. Follow this road over the next set of lights passing SAFEWAY
    supermarket on your left.

UTILITY ROOM

UP

HALL

DINING ROOM

'All the filming on the rig,' reiterates Sandy Johnson, 'was of exteriors. The trouble was the sunshine over the first two weeks: it looked like we were in Barbados and we couldn't have people think we'd cheated and shot the thing in the Caribbean. In the end, and hoping the weather would break, we shifted the more weather-reliant scenes to the end of the schedule.' And that was when the weather broke with a vengeance. 'We did all the night scenes and the shooting on the drill floor in the last week – including filming in the hurricane in the darkness.' That, says Sandy, was 'both exciting and dreadful'. Yet not, surprisingly, terribly difficult.

Difficulties arose in other, more unexpected areas. At one point the skies were being obstinately clear on a shoot when they desperately needed rain. Rain machines being not exactly two-a-penny on an oil rig, they improvised with fire hoses. 'Sea water,' says Sandy, 'was the only source and that was horrible.'

Horrible, of course, for the poor actors being sprayed.

'No, no. For the poor cameras and lighting equipment. Salt water is terribly corrosive; the cameras were in danger of seizing up.'

For Sandy, 'Roughnecks' carried with it an extra element of professional satisfaction. In most television series nowadays, there is more than one director. Sometimes this is due to other commitments, but it is more often because of the exigencies of time and speed. The norm as regards the amount of transmission time shot per day is four or five minutes. This may sound very little, but bearing in mind that there are often upwards of seventy scenes for fifty minutes of television, one begins to get the picture: each scene has to be prepared, read through, lit, voiced and often retaken. (And if that doesn't sound convincing, think oil rigs and hurricanes.) The way to speed-up this process is to have at least two directors 'leap-frogging': one is directing an episode while the other is editing the one just completed. But that is only possible if you shoot all the material for an individual episode in one go. In the case of 'Roughnecks', the opening scene of episode one was shot at the end of the twenty-one week schedule.

Sandy, therefore, directed all seven hours of 'Roughnecks'. 'Because I did the whole thing I like to think I put something of myself into this series. It was certainly a challenge because I'd never made anything with so many main characters – and I did some experimenting with shooting wide-angles. If you have two people in a scene it's pretty straightforward: you do one wide shot and two close-ups. But with ten people suddenly you've got ten reactions, ten times the dialogue and therefore potential for having ten times the number of shots. On that theory you'd have one wide shot and ten close-ups which is going to take a hell of a long time to do and also look pretty horrible. To get over that one I began to work more on choreographing numbers of people together so that I could do one shot with everyone in it, with the camera moving around finding moments within the scene, and having one point of view roping through the entire scene.'

Sandy them launches into director-speak. 'In film parlance I deliberately "crossed the line".' This has nothing to do with going to the equator but is a method of filming where you break the normal convention of keeping the camera in a line between the actors eyes in order that, from a viewer's point of view, they appear to be looking at each other. What is actually happening when you keep to the right side of the line is that one actor is looking camera left; the other camera right. If you cross the line in order to put everyone into the scene you have to be constantly aware of how you're approaching each actor and where they are looking so that the audience doesn't get confused. Readers may get confused – but no viewer has yet complained that the actors in 'Roughnecks' are looking the wrong way.

'Clint Eastwood,' says Sandy, 'crosses the line in movies like 'White Hunter, Black Heart' and his recent cowboy stuff. He's a really good exponent of the technique.' Pretty noble of Sandy to praise the man who stole his helicopter to go and play golf.

Rehearsing scenes before filming is something Sandy isn't keen on doing. 'I like to do a read-through in order that we get the whole picture, but often if you don't rehearse you'll get something, some sort of spontaneity that you'd never get otherwise. That,' he continues, 'is where casting is so crucial: my notion of casting is not so much to get someone to play the character but someone who *is* the character. That way, they're being much more themselves and anything they bring to the role should, within reason, be part of their character. Moira, Charles and I,' he adds, 'thought long and hard about the casting of 'Roughnecks', and generally took the creative decisions together – and usually let the actors experiment with their characters.'

Charles concurs. 'Originally, the characters of Davey and Kevin, for example, had no redeeming features at all. They were going to be really macho and utterly charmless. But when we auditioned Alec Westwood and George Rossi, they instantly brought a new dimension to the characters; they lightened them and gave them more depth. I mean, you don't exactly *like* them that much – but nor do you dislike them. They are, I reckon, a bit like naughty schoolboys.'

Ricky Tomlinson is full of praise about the way the producers and particularly Sandy let him develop the character of Cinders. 'I think we changed him a bit and made him far more humorous than he was originally. It really depends on the director on how much licence you can take with your character. Some are too scared to take a chance.'

One of the biggest problems in any production like 'Roughnecks' is the question of continuity. While the end-product looks, on-screen, extremely fluid, the actual process of filming is an endless stop-start activity using several locations and spread over a period of months. A scene, for example, that appears on television as two characters chatting as they move from the exterior to the interior of the rig is quite another story when it's being filmed. The exterior *is*, of course, the real exterior of the rig: the interior is a set at Bray Studios built three months later.

Actors and directors are used to this sort of thing, but it can pose problems on several counts. One is if the actor loses weight, has a haircut or generally changes his or her appearance in the interval between the two takes. It would look pretty silly if, in a scene which takes one minute of screen time and in which the actors are constantly in view, one of them suddenly gets afflicted by an alarmingly rapid slimming disease before our very eyes. Similarly, little details of their dress have to be noted by the continuity people. You don't want puzzled viewers wondering why our hero's shirt changed colour when he went indoors. That, then, is the reason why actors are photographed before each day's shooting.

Sandy outlines one of the other problems of continuity. 'It's difficult when you have, say, the rig supervisor staggering indoors out of the howling wind and rain. It means, three months later, we have to hire wind and rain machines in the studio so that the weather conditions, in the background of the shot, will still be the same. It's difficult for the actors as well; they may be beginning this scene half-way through the sentence they started when we were filming in Scotland. It's helpful,' he adds, 'that we have the cutting rooms nearby at Bray so that we and the actors in question can view the previous footage. It jogs their memories and helps get them in the right frame of mind.'

One of the costume team checking continuity

The most difficult part of shooting for everyone involved was, by common consent, the helicopter crash and subsequent rescue of the passengers. 'It was,' says Sandy, 'both brilliant and a nightmare: we used so many different sources.' Five locations were used to film what, on screen, looks as if it happened in the same place. There was the rig itself, the interior of the rig (Bray), Stonehaven harbour, a large pool at Romsey in Hampshire and another pool at Pinewood. And all were spread over the entire twenty-one weeks of filming. 'The shooting was so disjointed that I was pretty terrified about what it was going to look like when it came together.'

Roughnecks

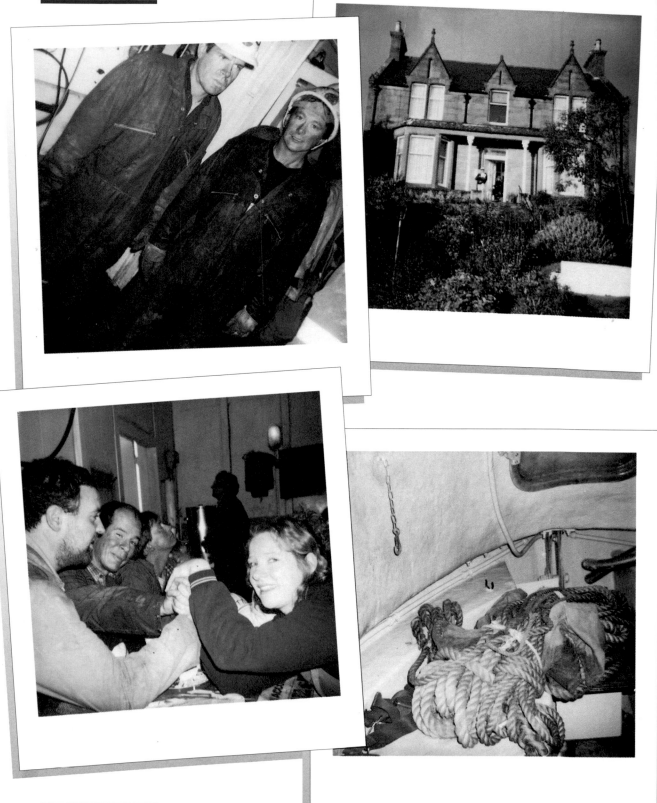

A selection of continuity
Polaroids

Charles Elton interjects with a story that proves once and for all that the camera really does lie. In this case, it told a real whopper. 'The Stonehaven stuff,' he says, 'looked dreadful when we viewed it. I mean, there we were, in a real sea, in the middle of a storm, with a real ship in the background – and it looked completely fake. It looked like we were in a studio.' It was, he goes on to explain, mainly because it was a terribly difficult scene to light.

The bizarre and ironic way of solving the problem was to reshoot the scene – at Pinewood. They used a big exterior surface tank, a wave machine, a rain machine; they made a model of a helicopter coming to the surface and then they painted a backdrop with a ship lurching about in the background. It sounds laughable – but it works a treat. To watch it no-one would ever know it wasn't shot in the middle of the North Sea. It probably helped that the actors really were wet and cold, exhausted and miserable. 'It was perishing,' says Charles, 'it was one of the last things we shot – and it was in the early hours of the morning.' Moira claims that 'watching those scenes being shot was the worst point of my career. I swear I'd never put anyone through that again.'

Sandy is disarmingly frank and extremely amusing about the post-production process; the endless editing that splices all these scenes together to make the final product. 'It's the most important time – and also the most depressing. You look at the rough cuts and think "this is rubbish". You just want to give up. So you then spend the next couple of months doing a lot of judicious editing – discreetly hiding your mistakes.' But Sandy's being a little too modest. He's highly experienced and well aware of the potential pitfalls in post-production – and in the case of 'Roughnecks' he knew that it would be impossible to reshoot any of the scenes on the rig. 'You have to be very aware of what you're getting while you're filming. We had the film developed and the rushes sent out to the rig so we knew, at each stage, exactly what we had. And we made sure we had masses of material. That way you can use the old maxim "if in doubt – cut it out".'

Sandy is blissfully unaware that he was very nearly obliged to cut out an entire day's filming. 'We lost the rushes from one of the days on the rig,' says Sam Mitchell, the producers' assistant. 'It was *awful*. But, thank God, we found them in the end. They'd fallen down the back of the fridge.' It's little moments like that when you identify with the glamorous world of television drama – it's awash with everyday dramas as well ...

One of the most vital elements of post-production – and one that can help make or break a series – is the decision about title music. With 'Roughnecks' they hit gold – the music was composed by the best in the business: Hollywood's Mike Post. He wrote the scores for – amongst other major hits – 'Hill Street Blues', 'LA Law' and 'NYPD Blue'.

'It was rather cheeky of us to approach him,' says Moira, dismissing the fact that her own name also precedes her. 'People in America queue up for him for years. We were very lucky to get him.'

Roger Neil, Mike Post's co-composer in Los Angeles and the man who did all the incidental music, sees it differently. 'We loved "Roughnecks" on sight. What's more, we developed a terrific working relationship with Moira and Charles. We were all in synch – I reckon we all had the same thing in mind.'

And what was that?

'A *big* sound – but with an element of sensibility to it. The show, after all, is about oil – oil is a giant. And it's about the sea, so we wanted a mythic sound as well. Our interpretation for the main title is a combination of elements; a sea shanty; electrical guitar with a big orchestral sound behind it and an elemental feeling to it.'

Mike Heron ex of The Incredible String Band, playing with his new group The Incredible Acoustic Band. Other members include John Rutherford, Stuart Smith and Dave Haswell

Moira, Charles and Sandy flew out to Los Angeles and together they worked further on the final theme tune and on a template for the incidental music all the way through the series. As Sandy says, 'spotting' the moments for when to have music is an important and delicate decision. It helps draw everything together and it accentuates and emphasizes mood and visual images. 'What Mike Post is particularly good at doing is in telling you when *not* to have music. A good composer knows when and when not to have music; when the drama is working without it. The last thing you want is for a composer to bang people on the head with overdone music.'

As for Roger Neil, the 'Roughnecks' experience gave him a chance to visit the land of his forefathers. 'There was definitely an element of "finding my roots". My grandfather's family came from Scotland and "Roughnecks" gave me the opportunity to visit the country for the first time in my life. And I got the full works! Helicopters, oil rigs, rough seas and all. It was great fun. Definitely the best show I've ever worked on.'

Moira describes the moment when Mike Post played the music as 'terrifying. What if it doesn't work? What if all those people who had told us to use a British composer were right?' Her fears were unfounded. 'The music was just perfect.'

And it's left a lot of producers green with envy. Aside from all the Americans queuing for Mike Post, it's very unusual for a British drama series to have people of Mike and Roger's calibre composing its music.

On the subject of music, there is a fitting epilogue to the making of 'Roughnecks' – and it served as both celebration, wake, and 'in joke' for the cast.

Ian Pollard, the ageing hippyish mechanic played by Paul Copley, was teased all the way through the series about his love for that late sixties musical phenomenon The Incredible String Band. And as Paul and not just his character loved the group's music, it became an off-screen as well as an on-screen tease.

And then, when Ian's death in the helicopter crash almost co-incided with the marriage of Heather Butcher and Chris Cassidy, an idea began to form in the producers' minds ...

They decided to make the wedding reception a celebration of marriage, of Ian's life – and a punch line to the String Band joke. They decided to get The Incredible String Band back together and have them play, on camera, at the reception.

Given that the group disbanded more than twenty years ago, this looked like an impossible task. Yet the production team behind 'Roughnecks' are nothing if not thorough in their research. Amazingly, they found that Mike Heron, one of the founders of the group, had formed another group called The Incredible Acoustic Band. Not only did they find the band, they persuaded them to play at the reception. So while Chris and Heather drive off into the sunset and while Ian's colleagues mourn his passing, viewing fans of Mike Heron get an extra treat. He is there, with his new band, singing the original hits of the original group. It was a total surprise to the cast of 'Roughnecks'.

But less surprising is the fact that Moira Williams, for all her talk of filming in the Paris Ritz, went on to make another 'Roughnecks' series. After all, she knows how to get the best out of her own incredible band ...

Pittodrie where Ian and Hilary's weekend and Heather and Chris's wedding was filmed. Pittodrie was chosen for the reception because Ian loved it.

The key cast relaxing in
the studio

▲

Crew roster

▼

CHRIS BRENNAN

'After we'd finished filming we met some journalists who asked me why Chris was such a bastard.' Liam Cunningham snorts and looks peeved. 'I was completely taken aback and deeply upset: I'm quite fond of Chris.'

Liam points out that the character of the volatile driller Chris Brennan has, in fact, a large moral streak. 'What the viewer is led to imagine is this line of blondes he's gone through but, when we first meet him, he's just been shafted by his girlfriend (she stole all the furniture from his villa in Spain) and then he spends the rest of the series trying to keep his colleague's daughter at bay. Then he ends up marrying her ...'

Liam makes it sound as if Chris is incapable of controlling his own life: an idea that his colleagues on the drill floor would laugh at. Yet here is the clue to the character of Chris: he has got his act together at work and knows exactly how to motivate his workers (sometimes by shouting at them), yet his personal life is a mess.

'People come up to me,' says Liam, 'and say "you shouldn't have married that girl. You're completely wrong for each other." It's extraordinary – and the first time that sort of thing has ever happened to me. I'm not Chris! But it doesn't make any difference. People who know me only vaguely are now deeply suspicious of me: they think I'm going to run off with their daughters ...'

Perhaps that also has something to do with the legends inscribed on Chris's hard hat in the series. On the front are the words 'Driller Killer' and on the back, 'I Drill Therefore I Am'.

Liam, famously, is the actor who likened an oil rig to the set of 'Alien' and described oil rigs as the most boring places under the sun. Does that mean he loathed the whole 'Roughnecks' experience?

Liam Cumnningham

'Far from it. It was – and I know this sounds desperately "luvvie" – one of the best experiences of my career. Everyone on that rig bonded so well and as for the real rig crew – they were great guys and I have tremendous admiration for them. They're all so different – aggressive, shy, the whole gamut – but they all have wonderful senses of humour and they're terrific at working together. But I couldn't do what they do. It's exceptionally hard work, it's open to all the elements and rigs are dull, horrible places. Within twenty-four hours you've seen everything there is to see. Awful. I don't know how they do it.'

Dublin-born Liam, one has gathered, isn't very keen on being cooped up in confined spaces. Perhaps this has something to do with his three and a half years spent in Zimbabwe in his previous incarnation – as an electrician. 'I spent a lot of time in a National Park the size of Belgium and I loved it. When I came home I knew I had to switch gear. Being an electrician in Dublin just didn't have the same glamour.'

'I've been in love with movies for years, and when my wife saw an ad for an acting school I thought I'd give that a crack and when I did ... well, it was like being hit by a truck. It really inspired me. That was it: I haven't looked back since. I've been tremendously lucky.'

He's also being tremendously modest. 'Luck' doesn't seem an appropriate word for an actor who, in only six years in the profession, hasn't stopped working. And much of that work has been in Hollywood. When pressed, Liam explains that it's just because he 'hasn't been found out yet'. Yet given that he's worked with David Puttnam and Mike Newell, starred in 'The Little Princess' and – with Sean Connery and Richard Gere – in 'First Knight', it seems the only thing to 'find out' is talent.

But Liam still has his feet firmly on the ground. Hollywood, he says, 'is like Dagenham. Everyone's in the business, In Dagenham they work in the car industry: in Hollywood it's the movies. *Everything* is about movies: it's an extremely bizarre place. But its movies are all about money: I'm even more astonished now than I used to be when I see a really *good* film coming from Los Angeles. I believe they made four hundred and eighty five last year. That,' explains Liam, 'puts a lot of pressure on the genuinely creative and artistic people. They're under so much pressure to make money that there's a real danger of the artistic side disappearing altogether.'

It was the creative, hands-on aspect of 'Roughnecks' that so appealed to Liam. He had great admiration for the producers and the way they let the actors develop their characters and also for the real rig crew in their willingness to guide the actors. 'Coming from a technical background, I really wanted to portray Chris's job as accurately as possible. Anyway, it was the first time that anyone had really looked into what these guys did and we couldn't afford to get it wrong. From the reaction we got from rig crews in Aberdeen, I think we got it right. But God, those oil rigs – they're lethal. I used to work in power stations and let me tell you they're like bouncy castles compared to rigs ...'

HEATHER BUTCHER

'When I was younger and visiting my aunt and uncle in Aberdeen', says Ashley Jensen, 'I used to *dread* taking the train back home. It was always full of drunk oil-rig workers carrying hard hats with silly things written on them and I can remember sitting in my seat praying "don't talk to me; don't look at me". Now, an older and wiser Ashley will be the first person to join in their conversations. 'I suppose I used to be slightly scared of them. Now I know they're just men getting excited because they're coming home after being cooped up in an oil rig for two weeks.'

Ashley's new-found knowledge comes from her role as Heather, the wilful and headstrong daughter of Tom and Izzy Butcher. Far from being wary of oilmen, Heather has spent most

of her life surrounded by them at Greenacres, the boarding house her parents run for the workers when they're onshore. 'Heather,' says Ashley of her character, 'is an only child and has grown up with all these men around her, bringing her presents and pampering her. While her parents are down-to-earth people, it's not surprising that she has grown up a bit spoiled – and a bit arrogant. You'd have to be a wee bit arrogant to think you could tame someone like Chris Brennan. Not only is he much older than Heather, but he comes with something of a reputation ...'

Chris Brennan, of course, is one of Heather's father's colleagues. Heather has known him since she was a child, but the relationship that develops between them as the series progresses is very much an adult one.

Ashley laughs when she mentions the love scenes between Heather and Chris. 'It was my first time – of playing that sort of scene! – and I suppose it would have been difficult if Liam and I hadn't got on so well. I suppose I was slightly apprehensive, but at the end of the day it's like any other acting experience and you just smile and get on with it. Anyway, you've got to remember that what comes over on the screen as Heather and Chris in an intimate moment is, in reality, Liam and me in a room with about twelve other people, lights and cameras.' Hardly intimate. Still, Ashley says that some of her friends said, 'Sorry, Ashley, I simply can't watch that episode.' 'They forget,' she says, 'that it's not *me* they're watching. It's Heather.'

So was that the most challenging aspect of playing Heather? 'Oh no. Heather may be younger than me (Ashley is in fact seven years older than her character), but there's one thing she can do that I can't – she can drive.' Ashley laughs when she remembers her first interview for the part. 'I was given these scripts and in nearly every one of Heather's scenes I read the instructions "Heather gets into her car." "Heather pulls away." "Close-up of Heather at the wheel".' I remember thinking: what do I say? Do I lose the job now, do I lie, or do I just keep quiet? Eventually I decided that if nobody asked whether or not I could drive, I'd just keep quiet. They didn't ask.' Two days later I signed the contract for the role of Heather. In the meantime, I'd been frantically driving round an industrial estate with a friend in a blind panic going "Oh God I can't *do* this!" But before we started shooting, I'd managed to do six proper lessons.'

Even so, Ashley was terrified when they filmed the first 'Heather pulls away' scenario. By that time, she'd come clean about her driving. 'They were brilliant about it,' she recalls. 'The art department mocked-up a set of L-plates and then they attached a camera to the dashboard and I drove off. I've never been so terrified in my life. It was dark, it was beginning to rain,

Ashley Jensen with Liam Cunningham

we were running out of shooting time and there I was, driving off with thousands of pounds worth of equipment in the car ... and I had to act at the same time!'

Yet Ashley's driving scenes passed off without mishap – except for the reversing scene. 'They cut that one.'

Yet, driving apart, filming 'Roughnecks' was one of the highlights of Ashley's acting career. 'I loved it. I loved the nitty-gritty realism of it. It wasn't all spectacle; it was very human in the way that it dealt with things that might seem little or unimportant but are actually vital and very big within the context of people's lives. I think I've been very lucky in my career,' Ashley continues, 'in that, while it's been mostly theatre, it's been vary varied. If there has been a tendency to typecast me it's been in comedy – as a dotty Scottish secretary. I've played several – both in theatre and television sitcoms like 'May to December', so playing Heather was a complete contrast. In the first series, Heather was nineteen and I was twenty-five. I think they wanted someone who was in fact older than Heather because she is actually wise beyond her years in that she knows what she wants and how to get it; she has the savvy to attract a much older man. On the other hand – and like most nineteen year olds – she didn't stop to consider the broader picture; her future and the likelihood of her being able to stay at college at the same time as holding on to an older man with a dodgy reputation who spends half his life offshore. All a lot more complicated than learning to drive.'

Ashley is in the fortunate position of being constantly in work while not having to make the move – as so many Scottish actors feel compelled to do – to London. 'I probably will – eventually – but don't feel the need to do so at the moment. Most castings happen in London but that suits me as I love the five-hour train journey down from Glasgow. It gives me time to myself without thinking I have to be rushing around doing something.' And it seems to have paid dividends. Ashley's train journeys have resulted in television roles in 'Down Among the Big Boys', 'Rab C. Nesbitt', 'The Bill' and 'Dreaming'. And her theatre work has taken her all over Britain in productions varying from the award-winning 'Carluccio and the Queen of Hearts' 'The Prime of Miss Jean Brodie' and the touring production of 'Rab C. Nesbitt.'

Any regrets? 'Well,' says Ashley, 'I never got to go onto an oil rig while we were filming 'Roughnecks' ...'

IZZY BUTCHER

'No, thank God. I didn't get out onto the rig. I'm frightened of those helicopters.' Annie Raitt is adamant about that one. 'You hear such ghastly stories about them.'

Annie plays Izzy, who runs Greenacres while her husband Tom – no stranger to helicopters – works on the *Osprey Explorer*. On the surface, Izzy's life seems mundane. Most of her time is taken up with making beds and cooking gargantuan meals to whet the limitless appetites of her husband's colleagues who constitute her clients. But, says Annie, it's what lies beneath the surface that drew her to the character of Izzy. 'I was keen to play Izzy because, while she's something of a nurturer and an earth mother, it's clear that she's also independent. It's an unusual part because normally, on-screen, you're either an independent feminist or you're staying at home washing dishes. Izzy's role shows that women in the kitchen have to be independent beings anyway.'

It's evident that Izzy's daughter Heather has inherited her headstrong, independent streak. And because Tom spends half his life offshore, Izzy long ago made the decision not to base her life exclusively round his. 'Greenacres,' says Annie, 'is really her baby. Something to fall back on if anything should go wrong.' In episode six, there's a very strong indication that things are about to go wrong in their marriage. 'Ah,' chuckles Annie, 'I don't think I'm going to tell you how they deal with that one. You'll have to wait and see.'

In real life, Annie admits that if anything went wrong there's no way she could do something like run a boarding house. 'I'm a hopeless cook. I create complete chaos in the kitchen and get into a real flap. I really admire people who can do it all seemingly without effort.'

Like Izzy?

'Like the props men. Thank God for them. All the roast beef and whatnot that Izzy produces looks pretty fantastic – it's just that it was nothing to do with me.'

Thankfully, it looks highly unlikely that Annie will ever have to fall back on an emergency career. Her acting life has been busy and varied ever since she started at the Theatre in the Round with fellow thespians Bob Hoskins, Robert Powell and Ben Kingsley. 'The amazing thing about 'Roughnecks',' she says, 'is that it was the first time since those days that I'd been amongst a group of people with the same feeling and intent; in a group where everyone involved – production and actors alike – really was involved. I know this sounds really hackneyed, but I just don't know how Moira and Charles did it. *Everybody* got on with each other.'

Annie did, however, have her reservations at first. 'When I went to the first reading in London I looked at the enormous cast and thought, God, how on earth are all these people going to manage to relate to each other? The fact that we all did was, I think, due to the complete absence of any "luvviness", competitive spirit or emphasis on "I, me and mine". That,' says Annie, 'is often the downside of acting, yet I do appreciate how actors can become very self-obsessed. Lady Macbeth, for instance, is a very obsessive role – but if you get too carried away and remain "in character" while you're walking down the street you're going to get carted off in a large yellow van ...'

There was, however, a point during filming where Annie thought she herself might get carted off. 'It was during the scene when I'm trying to comfort Clive (who plays crane operator Archie) about his ex-wife's accident. I'm trying to ask Clive why the caller who alerted the ambulance hadn't left his or her name. My line read "Why did they make the phone call anonymously" – but could I pronounce that last word? Oh no. By the fourth take I was getting desperate: I knew I'd never be able to say the word. Then inspiration – and improvisation – hit. I changed the words to 'Why didn't they say who they were?' Clive looked at me and, in what was supposed to be a sad moment, nearly fell apart laughing. Instead of a look of concern, I was wearing a look of "Haven't I done well?"'

'The worst moment of shooting, however, was near the beginning of the schedule. We were filming the bit of Heather's wedding when the bride and groom are driving away and we were all waving them off. We were getting further and further behind schedule for the day and it looked like we'd never finish. But we had to: they'd hired an expensive piece of camera equipment just for the day to whiz the camera away at the end of the scene. But we only had half an hour of shooting to go and we hadn't even started filming. Worse, I was in my light, flimsy dancing-about gear and it was the middle of November and completely perishing. You wouldn't believe how cold it was. I could feel dribbles of cold running down my nostrils. But we

Annie Raitt

managed: we filmed the whole scene, retakes and all, in half an hour – but it did seem impossible at the time.'

A sharp contrast to one of Annie's previous roles – as Rita Duckworth's mother in 'Coronation Street'. 'They rehearse during the week and do the filming at the weekend; three episodes in two days. Because I didn't appear all the time it meant I could fit Coronation Street round everything else.'

'Everything else' means writing as well as acting. Annie has a lot of experience in writing treatments and outlines for TV series and, in addition, she ran her own production company for five years. 'Looking back on it,' she laughs, 'it was the funniest thing in the world as I'm the least businesslike person in the world.'

Yet the business of acting has taken her from the RSC – 'one of the best jobs because you're not doing the same thing every night' – to numerous television credits including 'The Lost Tribe', 'The Stars Look Down' and Melvyn Bragg's 'A Time to Dance'. She has appeared at the National Theatre and the Young Vic, and her film career includes Mike Leigh's acclaimed 'Bleak Moments' in which she played the lead.

'I enjoy the balance of writing versus acting. I love the obsessiveness about writing, the way the day to day mundanities recede. And you're on your own. The major hassle for any actor is that you can feel your life is in other people's hands all the time. On the other hand, the experience of "Roughnecks" is a fantastic example of the camaraderie, generosity of spirit and honesty amongst actors.'

And Annie knows all about honesty. Although now based in London, she hails from Musselburgh, just outside Edinburgh. It's known as 'The Honest Toon', allegedly because of a story dating back to the seventeenth century. 'I believe,' says Annie, 'the story goes that the king was riding through the town and, without knowing it, dropped his purse. One of the townspeople picked it up, came running after him and handed it back.'

Unlikely or not, it's the sort of story that debunks the myth that all Scots people are mean with money. It's the sort of story Aberdeen could do with. For some reason that no-one has ever been able to authenticate, Aberdonians are unfairly renowned for being mean ...

DAVEY RAINS

Alec Westwood, who plays roughneck Davey Rains, is the only Aberdonian in the cast. And no, he isn't mean. Furthermore, he is generous in his praise of his home town. By a strange and circuitous route, it led him to his acting career. 'When I was thirteen I won a scholarship to Robert Gordon's College (a public school in Aberdeen). That was a fantastic experience – apart from the fact that they played rugby instead of football, and I hated rugby. It was only when a friend said to me that there was "an acting place" you could go to play football that I was able to play my favourite sport.'

The rest, of course, is history. Acting had never crossed Alec's mind, but from then on it became his life.

That 'Roughnecks', Alec's first major TV role, brought him back to Aberdeen was a strange and unlikely stroke of luck. That it also brought him onto the rigs was a double delight: to fund his way through drama school, Alec used to work offshore. He is, then, uniquely amongst the cast, qualified to speak of the authenticity of 'Roughnecks'. 'Yes,' he says, 'it was true to life. Although I play a roughneck in the series and I worked in catering when I was on the rigs, the portrayal of life offshore is pretty authentic. I still have a lot of friends in Aberdeen who work or worked in the North Sea and they reckon that ninety per cent of the stuff shown in "Roughnecks" is accurate.' Not bad for a series which, by the nature of its medium and the obligation to provide entertainment, could be forgiven for tampering with the truth.

So, given all these similarities, is there an element of the real character of Alec Westwood in the character of Davey Rains? Alec laughs. 'No, not really. For a start

Davey comes from Glasgow. An even greater difference is in their football teams: Davey supports Rangers while I myself am Aberdeen's greatest fan.' Alec goes on to point out that Davey's support of Rangers is actually a betrayal of his roots. 'Davey is a Catholic by birth, but he has a troubled background and, in an attempt to shrug it off, he lost his faith. Worse, the by-product of that was his switch of allegiance from Catholic Celtic to Protestant Rangers.' Switching sides, as any Scottish football fan will know, is an even more heinous crime than changing religious faith.

'Davey,' continues Alec, 'is one of the youngest characters in the series. He's a bit puppyish, a bit insecure. Sure, he flares up a bit – but he's not really violent. He's actually very loyal, very down-to-earth – a typical and very normal working-class Glasgow chappie. He's jovial and always telling crap jokes, and if he's a bit sexist – that's only a show for the lads. The macho stuff on the rigs is nothing more than that.

So with Alec's knowledge of Aberdeen and the rigs, did he have a head start over his colleagues in the series? 'Only to a certain extent. Obviously I'd flown in helicopters before and knew what life was like on a rig, but I think my greatest advantage was that I could speak the language.' By this, Alec means two languages: one being the technical one and the other, perhaps more importantly, being the Aberdonian dialect. Alec's abiding memory of the language barrier comes from his first stint offshore.

'This was about fifteen years ago and at that point there were still some Americans on the rigs. One day, in the canteen, someone dropped a whole plateful of food over the floor and the chef yelled to the American standing next to him to "give him a clout." The American looked really puzzled and just stood there gaping. "Give him a *clout*," repeated the chef. The American, realizing that the whole room was now looking at him in exasperation, shrugged and thumped the man in the face. The reaction wasn't quite what he had expected and it was only later that he realized that "clout" is the Aberdonian word for a dish-cloth!'

The 'real' roughneck helping Alec while they were on the rig was, like Alec, from Aberdeen. 'I kept looking at him,' says Alec. 'He looked incredibly familiar. it was only a couple of days later that I realized why – I was at school with him!' The final – and most extraordinary – coincidence of Alec's 'Roughnecks' experience.

But was there anything in the series that struck him as being completely inaccurate? 'Yes,' laughs Alec, 'they would never ban porn! Davey, my character, was the one who smuggled in the videos which led to the ban. In reality, it's anyway impossible to ban porn. If you can't sleep at night – and often you can't as it gets hot and claustrophobic with four to

Alec Westwood

a cabin – you go and watch TV. In the middle of the night it's all satellite and cable and lots of the channels show blue movies.' Yet Davey adds that part of the plot of that episode was to get the 'new boy' Village (Hywel Simons) into trouble – a highly believable exercise. Practical jokes on newcomers are part and parcel of life offshore as well as amongst actors. Yet Alec is keeping pretty quiet about one joke: the one played on him ...

'CINDERS' HUDSON

'There was a story,' says Ricky Tomlinson who plays 'Cinders' the wise-cracking taxi-driver and lousy cook, 'that a Dutch welder died whilst helping build the rig we were filming on.

Although that must've been nearly twenty years ago, stories like that don't disappear and, for the superstitious amongst us, they can be pretty spooky. Alec Westwood was spooked. Anyway, because I'm a bit of a practical joker, I found a welder's mask and put it in on a chair in his cabin while he was asleep one night. We attached a fishing line to it and threaded the line through a small hole in the wall to the next door cabin. Then we moved the mask.' Ricky chuckles at the memory. 'Let's just say Alec wasn't too thrilled.'

Ricky tells the story, both as an example of the jokes the cast played on each other, and of the fact that everyone joined in the fun. 'We were always doing things together,' he says. 'Everyone was involved in everything. It was great.'

Yet there was one aspect of filming that Ricky admits was anything but great. It was at the very beginning of the three-week shoot on the *Dan Countess*, during the filming of the helicopter crash that was to kill Ian Pollard. 'It didn't help,' says Ricky, 'that I couldn't swim. Well ... I *can* swim; I can splash about a bit and I'm much better at it out of the water than in, but in the middle of November in the North Sea in the early hours of the morning I don't think it matters whether you're a good swimmer or not. It was really, really cold. It was also a difficult and dangerous scene to film and despite the fact that we had frogmen all around us and an ex-SAS soldier on hand to advise – I panicked.' Ricky lowers his voice as he recalls an experience which is evidently still fresh in his mind. He doesn't know it – but everyone else at the scene remembers Ricky's heroism more than his panic. By common consent, this was a truly dreadful and frightening experience. A rescue launch was called out and filming was cancelled. The launch, in fact, wasn't needed, but it was touch-and-go for a while.

So one might imagine that Ricky, of all the cast and crew, would talk most of the dangers inherent both in filming and in the oil industry. But not a bit of it. While appreciative of the pitfalls of life in the North Sea, he maintains that the conditions surrounding his previous profession are infinitely more dangerous. 'I was a builder until I was forty. The conditions on oil rigs,' he adds with vehemence, 'are far superior to those on any building site in this country to this day. And the mortality rate in the building trade is higher than that in the mining and fishing industries put together. There's a death every week on a building site. It's absolutely dreadful.'

Yet for all that Ricky has seen and experienced, his sense of humour remains intact. During filming on the *Dan Countess*, he founded the 'Cod Club', the band of fishermen who fished every night over the side of the rig. 'There was £5 for the lad who caught the first fish,' he chuckles. 'No-one even got so much as a bite so I got the chef to smuggle me a fish from the kitchen and put it on the end of my line. After half an hour of pretending to fish I screamed that I'd got a bite and they all rushed over to see me pull this wonderful fish out of the water.' Everyone was fooled and Ricky won the fiver. 'Just as well,' he adds, 'that the fish didn't have any batter on it ...'

Ricky also organized the quiz nights and the competitions that helped make the sojourn on the *Dan Countess* such an enjoyable experience. 'Yes,' he says, 'I was invariably the quiz-master.' Again it's left to others to comment further. 'Ricky,' says Moira William's, 'kept us in stitches. He was brilliant.'

Roughnecks

'Moira is fantastic,' says Ricky. 'I have the most enormous admiration for her. Don't tell her this' – here he lowers his voice – 'she did play the prima donna sometimes but, d'you know, we rather *liked* that. Even so, she got no special treatment from me when I was quizmaster. Oh no.

'The great thing about 'Roughnecks', he continues, 'is that we were allowed to experiment with and develop our characters. That's not always the case with acting; it depends on the director. Some of them are too scared to let the actors take licence with their characters – but not here. Cinders, for instance, became more of a joker than he had been originally. I think it paid off. He's become something of a character in my hometown of Liverpool. People call me Cinders in the street and ask me what I'm cooking up next.'

Ah. The cooking. Aren't meals on oil rigs supposed to be five-star affairs?

'Well, yes,' concedes Ricky. 'It was a bit unfair to make Cinders a scruffy character and a rotten cook. The real chef on the *Dan Countess* was absolutely amazing. He could cook anything. And the standard of hygiene in the kitchen was superb.'

So has Ricky picked up a few tips from his stint as Cinders?

'No. I still can't even boil water. But,' he adds, 'I learned that the cook often has an unofficial dual role on rigs. He's a bit like the camp boss; everybody goes to him with their problems. And he's often the one who organizes quiz nights and so on. In that respect Cinders was an accurate portrayal.'

He was also accurate in that, onshore, he also had another role. While Ricky has never met a cook who worked as a taxi driver 'on the beach', he says that, yes, many of the men have jobs onshore. 'These lads,' he says, 'are so active that they have to do something onshore. It's quite common.' It is also indicative of the fact that the money earned offshore isn't what it used to be. If you are a non-skilled oil-rig worker, the money is good – but not brilliant. only the professionals are extremely well-paid. For everyone else, a little extra is often not just handy but necessary.

If Cinders is heading towards becoming a household name, it won't be the first time that Ricky has achieved such status. Even though he left the series five years ago, he is still known to viewers as Bobby Grant from 'Brookside'. Other TV work includes 'Boys From The Blackstuff,' the lead role in 'United Kingdom' and a detective chief inspector alongside Robbie Coltrane in 'Cracker'. He is a familiar face in Ken Loach's feature films, starring in 'Riff Raff' and – with fellow

Ricky Tomlinson

Liverpudlian Bruce Jones who plays Terry in 'Roughnecks' – in the acclaimed 'Raining Stones'.

Yet 'Roughnecks' remains one of his greatest memories. 'I wouldn't care,' he says with feeling, 'if we were trapped on that rig for twelve months. I loved it.'

KEVIN LAMB

'Every time I come to a crossroads in my life, it's got something to do with ice-cream.' This may sound like a remark made by someone who has been trapped on an oil rig for twelve months and suffered as a consequence. It is, however, a perfectly rational remark, and accurately describes the milestones in George Rossi's career.

'My parents are Scottish-Italian ice-cream people,' says George, who plays Kevin, the volatile derrickman in the series. 'I don't exactly come from what you'd call an acting family, but after school I trained in stage management and then went on to study at East 15 Acting School in Glasgow. That,' he adds, 'led to my first (second, if you count birth) encounter with the ice-cream trade. I was offered – and accepted – a role as the son of a Glaswegian ice-cream seller in Bill Forsyth's 'Comfort and Joy'. But my drama school didn't like that at all. It's a bitter and rather odd irony that, while ostensibly training me for what everyone knows is a precarious career, they actively discouraged me from accepting that role before I'd graduated. When I went back after filming the movie, they said I'd missed so much that I would either have to repeat my first year or leave! I left.'

That proved to be an equally wise decision. Immediately upon leaving, he landed a part in the 'Max Headroom' film and went on to forge a career with television credits encompassing 'The Chain', 'The Bill', 'The Monocled Mutineer' and 'The Singing Detective'.

George is also a founder of Fortuna Films and has directed a number of short films under this banner. Here is where his next encounter with ice-cream came in useful. 'I was in the Cornetto ice-cream ad. Yes – the singing one. That was me. The great thing about it was that it helped give me the financial freedom to take a year out and pursue my other passion – directing. The upshot was that I made a feature film in Italy with Michael

Elphick, Neil Morrisey and Jesse Birdsall.' Watch out for 'The Ballad Of Kid Divine'; it's nothing like 'Roughnecks' – and nor was the experience of making it.

'At one point,' says George of the latter, 'my stage directions read 'Kevin stands precariously on the monkey-board.' Given that a monkey board is a small metal platform over a hundred feet up the A-Frame of the rig and we were filming in a hurricane, I didn't have to do much acting to stand precariously! At Drama School they teach you "reality before theatricality": well I'm telling you can't get much more real than the sort of conditions we were filming in. Thank God for Brian Macdonald, the derrickman I was shadowing. He was brilliant – he worked with us on both series as he was a very good teacher. And if there's one thing you really need it's your training. There are cables everywhere on a monkey board. And if you hold onto some of them when the rig's in operation you can get your hand chopped off.' George can laugh about it now but the memories are still fresh in his mind – especially the memory of filming at night in a hurricane. 'It wasn't bad at first. It was a force-two hurricane and the sea was only swelling a bit. Then it got dark, the fog descended and the sea started churning like a cauldron. And where were we? Yes – on the monkey board. Both the cameraman and I were harnessed in, leaning out over the edge. He was an experienced mountaineer but even he was going green.

Roughnecks

Eventually we stopped filming when the hurricane hit force twelve. I think our "shadows" thought we were wimps. They said they'd still be working in those conditions.

'I'd never do it in real life. Filming was a fantastic experience but I wouldn't do that kind of work for a living even if I were desperate. Apart from the very real dangers, there's not much to do when you're off duty – and you end up getting claustrophobia in bunk beds with four to a cabin. I think there are normally about thirty-nine guys sharing eight toilets and communal showers – all with those metal floors. It's not exactly five-star luxury!'

As for the character of Kevin, George found him fun to play. 'Sure, he's a bit rough – but you could go mad out there. Kevin's a hard-drinking sort of guy and as there's no drink off shore he's got to let off steam somehow.

George Rossi

He works hard, but apart from that he's got no way of letting off steam. The only exercise he would be able to do is to walk around the heli-deck. As I said, you could go mad being trapped on a rig for two weeks.'

But George, like the rest of the cast and crew, had a break on dry land after six days. With everyone else, he headed straight for the bar when they reached Aberdeen. 'The trouble is,' he laughs, 'people say that when you're on the rig you don't notice the slight swell. Well, maybe not – but you do when you get back to firm terrain; you're swaying from side to side. You look drunk even before you've had a drink.'

TOM BUTCHER

'Oh yes. The slightest whiff of alcohol on your breath and you're bumped. Drink – and drugs of course – are strictly forbidden offshore.' James Cosmo knows whereof he speaks. He plays Tom Butcher, wife of Izzy, long-suffering father of Heather, and admin man and medic on the *Osprey Explorer*. He allocates the cabins, has all the rules and regulations at his fingertips, and dishes out the drugs: for medicinal purposes only.

'I learned about Tom's role from Ed the Med – the real medical officer on the rig. He's not a doctor, but is trained in advanced first aid to paramedic level. Yet, given the isolated locations of rigs, he's got access to stronger drugs than, say, an ambulance crew would have.'

This is all very well, but doesn't exactly inspire confidence. What happens if there's a severe accident or an illness that a paramedic couldn't possibly deal with? Isn't there a 'real' doctor on the rig?

'No. But the medic would immediately call air-sea rescue who come out in any weather.'

Any weather? Any *North Sea* weather?

'Well,' says James. 'They try ...'

And if they don't succeed it's up to the medic to deal with any accidents and emergencies. And the potential for accidents, despite the stringent safety standards, is enormous. As some of the actors were told, 'you're not a real Roughneck unless you've got a finger missing.' And they don't speak in jest: many roughnecks really have severed fingers and toes.

James is glad that he doesn't play the medic role in real life. 'I wouldn't like it at all. And I certainly wouldn't like to work on a rig. When we were filming on the drill floor in a force-twelve hurricane the rain was actually blowing upwards at one point! And then there's the complete lack of privacy. Dreadful. If you try to be on your own you end up with ten other people who are trying to be on their own too ...'

There was one point when James was justifiably desperate to get off the rig – yet couldn't because of the weather. 'My wife was about to give birth in a London hospital – and there I was, stuck in the middle of the North Sea. That,' he adds with emphasis, 'is an experience I would not like to repeat.' And, while everyone on the rig was delighted for him, they couldn't, of course, crack open the champagne. 'We celebrated with cocoa.'

But what of Tom's other role – as family man and the proprietor of Greenacres? Again, says James, that was highly realistic. He points out – as others have done – that the money on rigs isn't as good as it used to be and that Tom, being a canny Aberdonian, saw an opportunity to benefit from owning a boarding house. 'Tom has been on the rigs since day one –

since the seventies – and was quick to realize that prices in Aberdeen were about to escalate enormously. I reckon he bought Greenacres on a rising market and, with Izzy, realized they could use it as a money-making venture.'

If that had been the case in real life, Tom would have been one of the lucky few: in the late seventies and early eighties house prices in Aberdeen and its immediate environs rocketed and a house like Greenacres would have been worth the same as its equivalent in central London. But with the subsequent slump in the oil industry, a lot of property owners in Aberdeen got very badly stung. But then Tom, as James points out, is extremely canny.

Tom's relationship with his wife Izzy, which looks like falling apart at the end of the series, is again highly plausible. A lot of marriages have floundered because of the pressures of life offshore – and Tom has the added problem of his daughter marrying one of his colleagues. 'Tom is extremely proud of Heather,' says James, 'but she's like her mother: headstrong. I reckon Tom worries himself sick about her.' Again, like a true Aberdonian, he doesn't let it show.

Filming 'Roughnecks', says James, is one of the toughest roles he's had. 'The hours were long, we had little time off – and filming the helicopter crash in Stonehaven harbour was absolutely perishing; lots of immersion in ice-cold water. Yet it was the high-point of the series – a series I'm very proud of. I felt very committed to it: I've never done a TV series or a film with so many personalities and no arguments.'

Praise indeed from a man who followed in his father's acting footsteps at the age of seventeen. His television career dates back to series like 'The Sweeney' and 'The

James Cosmo

Professionals' while his early films include 'Black Beauty' and 'Young Winston'. More recently, he has been seen on the small screen in 'Casualty', 'Between The Lines' and 'Rab C. Nesbitt' and – immediately after completing 'Roughnecks' – he went on to film 'Braveheart' with Mel Gibson. 'That,' says James, 'involved four and a half months of sitting on a horse. Oh yes, I could already ride but I'm now a bloody good rider! Mel Gibson,' he adds, 'was terrific. He was both the star and the director and he's highly professional in both roles. No "I'm a Hollywood star" nonsense. He was extremely enthusiastic and had a really high quality team around him.'

Yet despite James's reservations about offshore life, he's hoping that 'Roughnecks' will be back.

IAN POLLARD

If 'Roughnecks' continues to roll, Paul Copley, alone amongst the cast, won't be there to enjoy the experience. He plays chief mechanic Ian Pollard, the only fatality of the helicopter crash. 'Yes,' he muses, 'I'm extremely sorry that I copped it, but of course I'd known the storyline from the start so it didn't come as a surprise to me.'

But Ian's death came as a horrible shock to his colleagues – and most of all to Hilary, with whom he was having a 'will they, won't they?' relationship. While Paul has never actually met anyone who had had a 'shipboard romance' on a rig, he acknowledges that women offshore are paid a great deal of attention. 'The men tend to use women as sounding-boards, as people on whom they can offload their problems.' And Hilary, in the series, certainly got her share of that. On her

Roughnecks

first morning at work offshore, she had six male visitors to 'see how she was getting on' and to offer her coffee. But for Hilary, they caused problems rather than sharing them.

'As a hands-on experience' (Paul is no longer talking about the romance), 'Roughnecks' is up there with the big films I've done. I love learning practical skills in my acting jobs so the job of mechanic was great. It's extremely stimulating and interesting to get an insight into someone else's skill. I spent a lot of time with the "real" mechanic, making sure everything I did was right. It reminded me of the time I was in Holland in "A Bridge Too Far" playing Anthony Hopkins' batman when I learned a lot about being a soldier.'

By a happy coincidence, Paul renewed his acquaintance with Anthony Hopkins shortly before the filming of 'Roughnecks'. 'I acted with him again in "The Remains Of The Day". He was great; a charming man and he clearly remembered our time in Holland.'

After 'Roughnecks', Paul got another insight into a rather different practical skill. 'I've just played a pathologist in "Cracker". Delving into people,' he muses, 'isn't that unlike being a mechanic. You're doing human mechanics, aren't you?'

One of the highlights of 'Roughnecks' was, for Paul, the opportunity to indulge in one of his favourite activities – riding motorbikes. In the series, Ian's passion is to ride through the Scottish Highlands on a 900cc Triumph; a role Paul had absolutely no problem in identifying with. 'It was fantastic. The scenery up there is spectacular and it was great to be riding a Triumph again. When I was eighteen I had a Triumph and, at that time, the model I had was the fastest bike in the world. To be handed a brand new bike during filming and to be told to "go and get used to it" was great. Funnily enough, I spent a lot of time getting used to it ...'

Ian was also lucky enough to do a lot of filming at Pittodrie House, a spectacularly beautiful mansion dating from the sixteenth century that was used for Ian and Hilary's weekend in the country and also for Heather Butcher's wedding to Chris Brennan. A consolation prize, perhaps, for copping it at the end.

As for the offshore filming, Ian found it 'an extremely exciting and exhilarating experience. Although,' he adds, 'it's also a bit like being in jail. Living in such close quarters with nothing much to do and no exercise apart from walking round the heli-deck. And it *was* scary at times. Climbing a hundred and twenty feet to the little platform up the derrick I froze for a minute and then looked down. Not a good idea.

Paul Copley

Everything's metal and there are all those little grilles so you can see everything below you ...'

For the real rig crew, Paul has nothing but praise. 'I think they were pretty sceptical when we first arrived and were expecting all sorts of minor accidents and getting feet stuck down holes and all that sort of thing. There's nothing, you see, that you can't bruise or cut yourself on. Yet as you know, the men on the rig turned out to be damn good company.

Sure, they are big, rough and tough, but what surprised me – perhaps it shouldn't have done – is that they're very bright and have a great many interests. They are as agile mentally as they are physically. People forget that a lot of the jobs offshore are intellectually demanding.'

Paul too has several intellectually demanding pursuits. As well as acting in film and television and theatre roles which have taken him to both the Royal Court and National Theatres, he also writes for both screen and radio. And to relax, he swims. 'That was another thing I was able to indulge in while filming "Roughnecks".'

That doesn't exactly sound like a whole bundle of fun in the North Sea in November. Anyway, Ian didn't swim – he drowned. Paul laughs. 'Well alright; it was less about swimming than holding your breath in twenty feet of freezing cold water. It was actually a very difficult scene to film.' And – after they'd reshot it at Pinewood – the last scene that Paul filmed for the series. R.I.P. Ian Pollard.

TERRY MORRELL

'We were all really upset at losing Paul Copley. It was a real shame. We miss him.' Bruce Jones makes it sound as if Paul, like his character, is actually deceased. (He isn't.) It's just that – like the rest of the 'Roughnecks' team, Bruce feels that losing Paul is like losing a member of the family.

Bruce's character is Terry Morrel, the O.I.M. or skipper of the *Osprey Explorer*, is the man ultimately responsible for the lives of the rig crew when they are offshore. And he would have had to account for the helicopter accident and the death of Ian Pollard. It's a hugely demanding job and one that Bruce learned from Dave Adams, the real skipper of the rig. 'I shadowed him for days – he was extremely helpful and I got a real insight into how the whole thing works; doing the rounds of the rig, checking all the machines, monitoring the waves and the ballast and all

Bruce Jones

that sort of thing.' Bruce has nothing but praise for Dave and his crew. 'They looked after us really well. Nothing was too much trouble.'

Real O.I.M.s have a luxury that Bruce himself didn't enjoy. Like the rest of the actors and production crew, Bruce shared a cabin with three others, but had he really been the skipper he would have had his own cabin with en-suite bathroom. A very real luxury, he admits, but not one that would entice him offshore in real life. Anyway, as he points out, he doesn't have the right background.

'Terry is ex-Merchant Navy. A lot of the more senior offshore people used to be in the Merchant Navy and, like Terry, were ships' captains.' Bruce, on the other hand, has been an actor all his life, having gone into the business straight from school. He has recently been part of the success of Ken Loach's award-winning 'Raining Stones.' During the filming of 'Roughnecks' he learned that he had been nominated as Best Actor at the Pescara Film Festival in Italy for his role in the movie and took a day off filming to fly to Italy to collect his award. When he returned, it was to be greeted by the news that he had been nominated for a similar award from the *London Evening Standard*. 'Yes', he says modestly, 'that film won a lot of awards.'

Getting off the rig for the brief trip to Italy was a welcome relief from filming in what had become increasingly appalling weather. 'We had just,' explains Bruce, 'filmed in a storm. John McGlynn and I had been doing a scene where we were climbing up those metal steps on the outside of the rig and we were getting absolutely *nowhere*. The wind was so bad that it got to the stage where I was pulling myself up, John was pushing me and still we didn't make any progress. It was actually quite frightening; I thought "Blimey, what on earth are we doing here?"

But in the end we managed to film the scene. But that night was definitely the worst moment of the whole experience.'

Bruce goes on to say that, the following morning, one of the 'real' rig crew said the Air and Sea Rescue had phoned the rig to ask if they all wanted to be evacuated. 'I thought they were joking – but apparently not. It really was a *bad* storm.'

Weather apart, Bruce thoroughly enjoyed his time aboard the *Dan Countess*. Like the rest of his acting colleagues, he relished the camaraderie that existed not just between the 'Roughnecks' people but among the rig crew as well. 'The whole experience was great – and the food was fantastic. It was a little cruel to the chefs on the North Sea to make Cinders such a bad cook!'

Eagle-eyed viewers will note that Terry wears a wedding ring in the series but there is never any mention of a wife. 'I think,' explains Bruce, 'that we're keeping his options open. No-one – not even he – knows if he's married, separated or divorced. The producer said that if anyone wants to have an affair they can have it with Terry. And he's willing to be played with ...'

But not in real life. Bruce is happily married and has, in fact, just been on holiday with Ricky Tomlinson: so it's all being kept in the family both offshore and on.

On the subject of the opposite sex, what about sexism on rigs? As the O.I.M., Terry is well aware that some of his crew don't exactly take kindly to having two women on board while others find it difficult to leave them alone.

'I never encountered any sexism and none of the O.I.M.s I talked to even mentioned it. I gather that if there's any "attitude" as regards women being offshore it's going to come from the crew – the O.I.M. has to be above that sort of thing. He can't afford to take sides either, or to let many feelings show. It's funny,' continues Bruce, 'but originally several people said 'play Terry like a real bastard; a mean, hard sort.' I wasn't happy with that and went to the real O.I.M. who said 'definitely not. That wouldn't be realistic.' And of course he was right; you can't afford to be antagonistic or to rub people up the wrong way. After all, you're stuck on that rig in the middle of the North Sea and nobody can get away from anyone else no matter how much you might want to ...'

ARCHIE McGRANDLE

'I loved it because I enjoy being on my own most of the time.' This is a first. Is Clive Russell, who plays Archie the crane operator, talking about the same series as everyone else? You know, the one where you're all cooped up in a metal thing in the middle of the North Sea?

Clive laughs at the question. 'Yes, I know it sounds odd to say that I could be on my own – but I *could*. As a crane operator you're sitting there high up in solitary splendour: I'm happy with my own company and there's something very delightful about being in the cabin of the crane way above the North Sea. What's more, it's very exhilarating actually operating the crane. When you pick something up you can't let it sway from side to side: it's a very delicate manoeuvre for such an enormous piece of machinery.'

Clive, it would appear, is not untypical of the sort of man who becomes a crane operator in 'real life'. His professional counterpart on the rig also enjoyed being on his own, and indeed shares Clive's fairly solitary hobbies of golf and fishing. 'And,' adds Clive, 'he used to be a long-distance lorry driver.'

Yet while Clive also enjoyed the social dimension of life on the rig as well – the game-playing, the quizzes and the competitions – he points out that for someone who needed to be doing different things every day and talking to new people all the time, life on a rig must be very difficult. 'The boredom would be worse than anything, I think.'

Archie, however, differs greatly from Clive in one respect: he loves rabbits. In Episode One they find that a rabbit has found its way into one of the pipes being taken out to the rig, and it's Archie who bonds with this stowaway. 'We have two rabbits at home,' says Clive. 'I must say I'm not overly fond of them. And the rabbit in "Roughnecks" was actually two rabbits. One of them was docile and well-behaved but the other one – Barney – kept biting me. I had to get very strict with him. Also, I was convinced he grew over the duration of the three weeks we were on the rig. The props men kept insisting that he remained the same size, but I was sure he grew by as much as thirty per cent.' Viewers take note.

One of the most memorable scenes from 'Roughnecks' comes at the end of that episode when Archie, alone on the outside of the rig at night, cradles the rabbit in his arms and sings to him. Clive grins at the memory. 'It *was* a great scene, wasn't it? Actually, that scene was nominated by a television critic in London as his third-favourite "TV moment" of the year.'

Clive Russell

Part of the appeal of the scene is the quality of Clive's voice; but all he will admit to is the ability to 'hold a tune'. 'I'm an actor who can sing rather than a musical actor. Yet what was quite unusual about that scene is that it was all done there and then: the singing bit didn't have to be revoiced in a studio afterwards.'

Although born in Winchester, Clive grew up in Fife – but not in an acting family. His father owned a shoe shop in Leven and Clive was the first in the family to become a thespian. He has played a wide range of parts both in theatre and television, working extensively for the Royal Shakespeare Company and the Royal Court Theatre as well as in numerous television roles in series including 'Middlemarch', 'First Among Equals', 'The Bill', 'Casualty' and 'Cracker'.

But, at six foot six and with a Scottish accent, does Clive ever get typecast as just a 'big Scotsman'?

'Only to a certain extent. Being large *is* limiting in some ways, but being Scottish isn't. Anyway, I live in London and I think it's Scottish actors who live in Scotland who suffer. Yet casting for film and television is often pretty conservative but it obviously does help if the way you look reflects your character type, and I'm never going to look small! But that in itself can be an advantage: last year I played a Nova Scotian character in a movie with Helena Bonham Carter. She's very tiny and they wanted someone tall to play opposite her.'

Clive certainly seems to have avoided being cast as big, brutish and brawny. In 'Roughnecks', the sensitivity of his character – the rabbit apart – is at times painfully drawn in the scenes where we witness his inability to come to terms with his divorce and his wife's subsequent remarriage. These, combined with Archie's efforts to seek oblivion through alcohol while onshore, are some of the most poignant moments of the whole series. As Clive says, 'I've been very lucky with my storylines.'

CEEFAX

Ceefax Revell isn't interested in luck: it's knowledge he thirsts after. 'Yes,' says Colum Convey who plays the easygoing roughneck, 'he knows everything, doesn't he? In a way he's an oddball. He's highly intelligent, obviously well-educated, yet he's in his mid-thirties and he's still a roughneck. I reckon he's actually a bit of a disappointment to himself. He had the opportunity to do something with his knowledge and his education – but didn't have the bottle to follow it through. Still, at least he's a nice guy: my usual stock in trade is to play nasties.'

Irish-born Colum goes on to say that after playing a meanie in 'Middlemarch', a bad guy in 'Soldier Soldier' and various borderline psychopaths and hard-faced cynics in 'The Chief', 'The Bill' and other television and theatre parts, Ceefax was a joy. 'He's a compassionate guy and often acts as a buffer to the more volatile members of the crew.'

Colum found his time offshore extremely interesting, but 'I wouldn't do it in real life no matter how much they paid me. It's an extremely hazardous environment and very, very hard work. And if you lose your concentration for even one minute you could end up losing a finger as well. What you've got to remember is that none of us came anywhere near what it must really be like putting in a twelve-hour shift on the drill floor. If you're a roughneck on your first day offshore I reckon by the end of it your arms would be practically pulled out of their sockets. These guys have to be incredibly fit.' Another hazard for a new worker, he adds, is finding your way around the rig. 'Although they're actually very small, everything's at right angles and there are all these corridors. You spend the first day or so getting completely lost. If you try to get from A to B you usually end up back at A.'

But despite the fact that Colum would view the life of a roughneck as 'something like a prison sentence', he has tremendous admiration for the people who worked on the *Dan Countess*. 'They're very bright men and all perfect gentlemen. Watching the roughnecks work is, funnily enough, a bit like watching a dance being choreographed. Although everything is on a mammoth scale, they all work in synch and extremely quickly. Given that the screwed-together sections of pipe are ninety feet long and the sea bed is God knows how many thousands of feet below you, imagine how many pipes these roughnecks have to put together – and then haul apart – in order to drill?'

But the roughnecks don't have the luxury of leaving that to the imagination.

Colum's abiding memory of filming the series is the sequence in Episode Five when he and George Rossi (Kevin the derrickman) break out into a rendition of 'Bohemian Rhapsody'. 'It was completely spontaneous and unscripted. We were waiting for a lighting set-up and, out of sheer boredom, George and I started singing. Sandy Johnson decided to film us which we thought was just a bit of fun. But we should have known that something was up when everyone else got up and went behind the cameraman: they all knew that Ricky and James had hatched a plan to burst in with a fire extinguisher and turn it on us. We, of course, hadn't a clue. So our shocked, open-mouthed reaction, on film, is about as genuine as you can get. It was a complete surprise to us. For about three days afterwards,' he adds ruefully, 'I was tasting whatever sort of liquid it is they put in fire extinguishers.'

But it wasn't the taste of the liquid that prevented Colum from getting to sleep at night: it was yet another unscripted episode – and again Ricky and James, joined by Clive Russell, were the culprits. 'I was sharing a cabin with the three of them. Don't ever do that,' he counsels good-naturedly, 'they all snore something rotten!'

But Colum should be used to sleepless nights by now. His daughter was born after filming 'Roughnecks' and, he says in awe, 'you wouldn't believe that such a tiny creature could be capable of making such a racket.' Come back Ricky, James and Clive: all is forgiven.

Colum is still slightly surprised to find himself as an actor. 'I acted in plays at school and then in the local amateur dramatic society, but to be honest I always thought acting was the sort of thing that posh people did. But then a friend of my father's suggested I try it professionally so I thought "what the hell?" and applied to RADA. I got in first time!'

Colum hasn't looked back since, although he admits to being envious of one of his fellow actors in the first professional part he ever had. 'It was his first job as well so we were in the same boat. His name was Kenneth Brannagh.'

Colum Convey

TESSA BUCKINGHAM

'I *loved* being on helicopters – it was my favourite part of the whole job. I'd jump at the chance to go on one again.' And after playing Tessa the mechanic, Teresa Banham could probably mend a helicopter if anything went wrong. 'I really got into it,' she says. 'I can really see the appeal of that sort of job. I love practical things anyway; problem-solving and D.I.Y. And the real mechanic on the rig was incredibly helpful and accommodating. I plied him with questions and he ended up teaching me a lot.'

So much so, in fact, that after filming Tessa pursued her new-found interest, learned a great deal more about machinery and is now something of an expert on car mechanics. 'I've been able to do a lot of work on my own car and now, if ever I have to go into a garage, nobody tries to pull the wool over my eyes!'

Teresa Banham

So playing the feisty Tessa was a completely different kettle of fish from Teresa's award-winning previous role – as the tragic Anna Karenina in a touring theatre production. Poor old Anna's only encounter with things mechanical was with the train under which she eventually threw herself.

'But it's good to do both theatre and television. Although I thoroughly enjoyed the whole "Roughnecks" experience it becomes difficult, towards the end, to maintain the same degree of excitement and energy as you started with. With a five-month shoot there's inevitably a great deal of sitting around and waiting and you find you have to galvanize yourself into action. Theatre provides a nice contrast: it's more scary and it really gets the adrenalin going.'

Not that there weren't a lot of scary moments during the filming

of 'Roughnecks.' 'Yes; some of it was really tough and there were frightening moments, but what was good about those bits was that everyone clubbed together and pulled each other through. It was a fantastic bonding experience.'

The character of Tessa, however, is not as open as the actress who plays her. She's at something of a watershed in both her career and her emotional life and, perhaps in consequence, is quite guarded with her fellow employees on the rig – even with her room-mate Hilary. Part of the reason for this is, of course, that she is having a clandestine affair with the rig superintendent, Drew McAllister. She can hardly let slip to everyone that she's the boss's mistress: she has to prove herself on her own terms. 'But she's also naturally just a bit of a dark horse,' says Teresa, 'and it's a character trait that I liked in her; she remains something of a closed book. Also, she was escaping from something; from her onshore life and, in a way, from Drew. Perhaps a lot of people who choose to work offshore in preference to on land have something they want to escape from.'

Tessa's troubles are compounded in Episode Two when she is 'volunteered' to act as a temporary replacement chef – and serves up a truly disgusting meal. Teresa laughs at the memory. 'Oh, I had no difficulty with that bit. I would have made a real pig's ear of it in real life as well. Cooking is not my strong point.'

What is it with actors? Can't *any* of them cook?

They can, however, eat. Teresa joins her colleagues in praising the quality of the food offshore. 'It was terrific; three wonderful meals a day – and the chef was always baking cakes and shortbread as well. The food issue nearly caused a rather embarrassing problem because, before we started filming, we were all measured for dry-suits for a scene that, in the end, wasn't filmed. It was just as well because after three weeks of oil-rig food, we were all about half an inch bigger ...'

On the *Osprey Explorer*, Tessa was one of only two women doing what have traditionally been perceived as men's jobs in men's environments. Is it, then, also a sexist environment? 'I honestly don't know. We were treated very much as what we were – a film crew. And, on the production side, there were lots of other women on the rig so it was never a case of – as it seemed on camera – just Hilary and Tessa amongst all those men. But,' adds Teresa, 'after a while one did begin to get the feeling that, if there were no women in the recreation room, the men would be playing different sorts of videos ... Also, both we actors and the real crew were on our best behaviour. It would be interesting to know what it would be like if they had really let their hair down. Perhaps I'll have to go back in real life; go in undercover and get a job as a mechanic ...'

In 'real life', Teresa has actually been back to one of the Scottish locations. 'I went back to spend a weekend at Pittodrie House where Heather and Chris's wedding reception took place. It's absolutely beautiful and the countryside is stunning. And the food is wonderful ...'

HILARY WHITESON

'I think,' says Francesca Hunt, 'that part of the reason why our *doppelganger* crew were so willing to help us was because of the safety aspect. You know, they had to know what we were doing.'

And what Francesca, in acting the part of Hilary the mud-logger was doing, was one of the most responsible jobs on an oil rig. 'Before we started filming I was sent to a company in Aberdeen to learn about mud-logging. Apart from being fantastically interesting, it was great for the ego to be told that I was doing the most responsible job on the rig. I must admit I lapped it up ...'

Francesca, an Oxford graduate in philosophy and politics, went into acting after 'trying very hard *not* to. I'd done a lot of acting at Oxford but I thought I'd hate the "luvvie" aspect of doing it professionally. I thought I'd go into politics instead. That's standing up and acting anyway, isn't it?'

Yet Francesca found herself applying to Bristol Old Vic, was accepted – and hasn't looked back since.

'One of the most interesting times at

Bristol was when two of us participated in an exchange with the Moscow Arts Theatre School. That was fantastic: their devotion to acting is incredible and it was the first time I'd ever been told what a privilege it is to be an actor. In this country,' jokes Francesca, 'you're looked down on, sort of spat on and perceived as a bit odd. There, they take it all extremely seriously. And they didn't have an easy life. When we were there, *Glasnost* was just beginning and, while there was a lot of hope around, most of our fellow actors lived in absolutely minute apartments – sometimes one room – with their husbands, wives and children, subsisting on meagre student grants. And everyone was married! Even the eighteen or nineteen year olds.'

Francesca herself has recently married and – if ever any proof was needed that the cast of 'Roughnecks' became like a large family – many members of that family found that their professional commitments made it possible for them to attend her wedding.

Francesca was glad that everybody on the 'Roughnecks' set took life on a rig so seriously. As gutsy as the character she plays, she loved doing the survival and training courses – and adored being on helicopters.

'I loved them, but boy do you know you're flying. Helicopters really use the air; they drift, they get buffeted, and they fly so *low*. On one flight we encountered this thick fog that hangs about thirty metres above the sea. The only way to negotiate it is to fly underneath it, just above the waves. That was exceptionally exciting.'

Francesca, while having many theatrical credits to her name, made her television debut in 'Strathblair', the fifties farming saga also set in Scotland. 'We filmed in Blair Atholl in the highlands. That was breathtakingly beautiful, so it was a treat to get back to Scotland to do "Roughnecks". The countryside,' she adds, 'where we filmed Ian's and my weekend away on the motorbike was also stunning. I had no idea how beautiful Aberdeenshire is, nor how many enormous houses and wealthy estates there are around there. There are a lot of rich people up there.'

Well yes – and some of the money comes from oil. The oil found by people on rigs. 'Mmm,' says Francesca, 'I actually loved being on the rig, but they're so *small*. I don't know; maybe they're about two hundred yards square, but a lot of it is out of bounds. And I think the claustrophobia could get a bit tricky – especially if you're the only woman offshore. I met a female driller in Aberdeen who said it could get really lonely if you're out there on your own.' Especially if – like Francesca – you celebrate your thirtieth birthday offshore. 'Oh but that was great. They gave me a party and baked a cake. The only problem was: no booze! Nightmare.'

Francesca Hunt

One of Francesca's most vivid memories of 'Roughnecks' is of a night-time swimming survival course in Stonehaven harbour. 'It was freezing, snowing heavily – and Stonehaven was an hour's drive from where we were staying onshore. Teresa was supposed to be doing the course with me but her flight from London was delayed and, given all the circumstances, I thought "Oh thank God, I don't have to go". I was wrong. The instructor phoned and said I was still coming, wasn't I? It was more of a challenge than a question.'

So Francesca went. After an hour of skidding on icy roads she arrived at the harbour, was greeted with a "hello, here's your wet-suit", and plunged into the freezing water. 'It was quite extraordinary. I'm not particularly brave and I don't know how that man managed to get me to go swimming in the North Sea in the snow in the middle of winter.'

Sounds gruesome.

'No! It was wonderful!'

'VILLAGE' GRANELLI

'I reckon Village got off pretty lightly,' says Hywel Simons of the character he played in 'Roughnecks'. 'I heard some real horror stories about what happens to the new roustabouts on rigs ...'

Being given the nickname of Village (short for village idiot) and being teased relentlessly doesn't immediately spring to mind as a lucky escape, but when Hywel elaborates on the tricks played on new roustabouts, one begins to see what he means. 'The most common story I heard from people I talked to in Aberdeen,' continues Hywel, 'was about roustabouts being told to go into one of those huge metal containers they use on ships and rigs and clean it. Once the new boy's in, the door is closed behind him, the container is hoisted up by a crane and then dropped about twenty foot. Then a hose is attached to it and turned on full blast. The terrified guy inside thinks he's been dropped into the sea ... I don't think a character as eccentric as Village would actually survive on a rig.'

But survive he did even though, like several of his colleagues, he almost perished in the helicopter crash.

'Training for that at the RGIT Survival School,' says Hywel, 'was a nightmare; one of the most frightening things I've ever done. It was that

Hywel Simons

Roughnecks

helicopter simulator. To be put underwater, turned upside down and strapped in goes against every instinct you've got. I used to be a surfer in Wales and I knew from experience that once the water flushes up your nose you lose all sense of which way is up and which is down – your brain goes haywire.'

Ah. Wales. So does Hywel, like his character, come from a village in Wales?

'No,' laughs Hywel. 'I come from Porthcawl. It's a town on the mid-Glamorgan coast.'

And a town that has spawned, it turns out, a disproportionate number of actors. 'I had this drama teacher at school who was something of a guru – he's seen dozens of people into the profession, and it's thanks to him that I'm an actor. I was going to leave school at sixteen but he persuaded me to stay on and then to go to drama school.'

That drama school was LAMDA, the London Academy of Music and Dramatic Art, where Hywel played a wide variety of roles from the title role in *Macbeth* to Mr Pumblechook in *Great Expectations*. He is still slightly amazed that, a mere three weeks after graduating, he landed the role of Village in 'Roughnecks'. 'It was amazing, and whatever happens, I'll never forget my first job. I'll probably have the best memories of any actor of my generation.'

So, while Hywel – like his character – really was 'the new boy', it seems that actors are a kinder breed than fictionalized roughnecks. Hywel got no flak for being a beginner. 'On the contrary. Everyone was incredibly helpful and it was really nice to get tips about acting in front of a camera. I'd never done it before.'

Hywel does admit, however, to being fleeced at poker on a regular basis while they were living on the rig. And – perhaps the only other similarity between him and his character – he was completely taken in by Ricky Tomlinson 'catching' the fish that he had actually smuggled up from the kitchen.

On the subject of kitchens, Village's final acceptance by his colleagues came after his unexpected success as a temporary chef during Cinders' absence. And unlike Annie Raitt, Ricky Tomlinson and Teresa Banham who unanimously claim total ineptitude in the culinary department, Hywel actually can cook. 'Oh yes. I love cooking. There's a strong tradition of cooking in my family – my mother's terrific and I've actually worked as a waiter, barman and chef in the past, so, yes, I suppose I do break the rules about 'Roughnecks' actors being hopeless in the kitchen.'

Hywel, like Francesca Hunt, celebrated a birthday during the filming of 'Roughnecks'. Yet while Francesca spent hers on the rig on a clear, starry night, Hywel had an altogether less pleasant time of it. 'It was on the very last day of shooting when we were actually in that outdoor tank behind the studios at Bray finishing the crash scene. It was in the middle of winter and absolutely freezing – the coldest night of my life. And we were filming at four in the morning when you're at your lowest ebb.'

Sounds fun.

'Memorable, anyway. We were wearing four layers of thermals under our survival suits and also a layer of tin foil next to our skin to try to keep the warmth in.'

And did that work?

'No. But the whiskies did.' Hywel laughs when he remembers going back to the hotel after they'd finished shooting at seven in the morning. 'They opened the bar specially for us. You should have seen the looks on the faces of the other guests as they came down to breakfast and were greeted with the sight of exhausted, bedraggled actors wearing survival suits and knocking back the booze ...'

Yet Hywel relished the whole 'Roughnecks' experience and reckons he was incredibly spoiled to have cut his professional acting teeth on such an enjoyable series. He also loved playing the part of Village – even if the role did rub off on him to some extent. 'When the whale was first sighted below the rig,' remembers Hywel, 'someone rushed into the rec room and yelled 'Whales!' I immediately thought they'd said 'Wales' and were talking about me ...'

DREW McALLISTER

'There's hope for me yet,' says John McGlynn. 'Despite playing the role of Drew, I haven't been typecast as a bad guy. Although,' he adds with a wry smile, 'I did then go on to play an emotionally inadequate dentist who beats up his Aids-suffering brother in a 'Screen Two' production ...' The dentist, as John goes on to explain, was 'a total bastard. Drew is just a bastard.'

A fine distinction, no doubt.

A more polite way of putting it is that the 'Roughnecks' Rig Superintendent Drew McAllister is perhaps the least sympathetic of the characters in the series. He messes his wife around by having an affair with Tessa, and he messes Tessa around by playing the age-old game of 'I'm going to leave my wife. Soon.' He's none too charming to the crew of the *Osprey Explorer* either; yet, as the man in charge of the rig's budget, he's got a good excuse for being tough.

John himself insists that he's the exception to director Sandy Johnson's rule of 'casting to type'. 'I played a nice guy in 'Soldier Soldier' just before I did 'Roughnecks' so I can't be all that bad. Mind you, it's much more interesting playing a bastard in a suit ...'

Edinburgh-born John's television credits bear out his versatility. Probably best known to viewers as Calum Buchanan in 'All Creatures Great And Small', he has also appeared in series including 'Jute City', 'Casualty', 'Dr Finlay', 'Lovejoy', 'Tutti Frutti' and 'Taggart'. Additionally, he has various radio credits and has narrated several 'Without Walls' documentaries for Channel 4. Outside acting, he was – and is – a professional jazz drummer: a career which led him to acting. While he still wants to keep his musical career going, he says that it's very difficult for anyone to make a living as a live musician doing gigs in this country. 'Playing in pubs is difficult: most of them only have a license for a duo, and also the public now expect live music to sound perfect. It doesn't. And anyway, pub culture in this country isn't really suited to live music anymore.'

But, going back to 'Roughnecks', was John suited to life offshore?

'Oh it was great. I wasn't on the rig as much as the others, but doing "Roughnecks" was a fantastic experience. And I'll never put petrol in my car again without thinking of the people who work on those rigs. In my ignorance, I had expected them to be a bunch of (the next bit is unrepeatable), but I stand corrected – and humbled. Those guys are brave, clever and strong and I felt pretty small next to them. At one point, I actually felt embarrassed by my ignorance of their world.' In that respect,

John McGlynn

Roughnecks

John didn't have the same advantage as many of his colleagues who were 'trained' for their roles by their real-life counterparts. 'I just had to be there, shouting at someone over the phone or in the office, wearing a suit and being a bastard ...'

Yet at one point John donned overalls over his suit and joined the others in filming the most memorable scene: the scene on the rig in the storm. In consequence, he is now a member of the 'Force-12 Club', a society exclusive to those who have filmed on an oil-rig in a Force-12 gale. 'Imagine,' says John, 'being stranded on twenty thousand tons of metal rolling about in the sea. Interesting. We thought it was bad enough as the rig listed about three degrees off vertical, but the guys who worked there said the structure can tilt as much as eight degrees in a really bad storm. Apparently,' adds John without envy, 'that's like being in an office block which is behaving like a rowing boat.' Then he laughs as he remembers the practical difficulties of filming on that occasion. 'It was very very cold and raining extremely hard. The trouble was, the wind was so strong that the rain was blowing left to right instead of up and down. The real rain just didn't look real: viewers would have thought the cameraman had dropped the camera or something so we had to use visual-effects rain to make it look vertical.'

Another fascinating example of the camera being obliged to lie.

And talking of lying, what does John think of Drew's behaviour towards his wife and Tessa?

'Cowardly,' says John without hesitation. 'Yet, because no-one was sure whether or not we would go on to do a second series, the character of Drew couldn't really develop. He was established as a person, yet his marital situation had to remain unresolved, so he didn't grow as a character. That's my only regret about 'Roughnecks'; the fact that you never really got a deeper insight into Drew. Apart from that it was a tremendous experience: I was working with people I could really trust. It's not always like that in TV.' John goes on to relate a story about a well-known television series: a story that involves people behaving infinitely worse – in real life – than the fictional Drew could ever manage.

But if John was sad when it was all over, he was glad in another respect: he had an opportunity to exercise his musical talents. 'At the wrap party when we'd finished filming, Race Davies (the actress who played the visiting journalist) and I got together – she on the cello and me on the drums – and performed an impromptu gig. That was great. We even played a rather odd version of the "Roughnecks" theme tune ...'

Mike Post, the Hollywood supremo who composed the real tune, is unavailable for comment on that one.

▲

Shift Rota

▼

EPISODE ONE

The rig crew of the *Osprey Explorer* are in Aberdeen ready to fly out to the North Sea. Most of them are old hands: two of them are new. One of the latter, mud-logger Hilary Whiteson, is a late transferral to the *Osprey Explorer*. The other, cocky Wilf Granelli, gets off on the wrong foot with everyone – even with the prostitute he tries to pick up in an Aberdeen pub. He also, and very unwisely, tries to make out that he has been offshore before. Dressed in a stetson and cowboy boots, it's evident he's going to have a lot to learn about life – and especially life offshore ...

The others are veterans of the lifestyle, used to the two week on, two week off cycle. Yet Chris Brennan, the lady-killer driller, has had a particularly unhappy two weeks onshore: Stacey, his young girlfriend (of very short standing) has removed thousands of pounds worth of furniture from his house in Spain. As some of the crew gather at 'Greenacres', Izzy Butcher's boarding house, before the helicopter flight to the rig, their attitude is very much 'it serves you right'. Ceefax the roughneck jokes that Stacey will have sold the furniture 'to buy sweeties'. Chris is not a happy man.

Gentle giant Archie the crane operator isn't happy either: he still cannot accept the fact of his divorce, his ex-wife's custody of their two children, and her subsequent remarriage. He has taken refuge in drink and the only way he managed to make it to 'Greenacres' is because 'Cinders' the rig cook is, while onshore, a taxi-driver, and spotted him at the station.

Two days later it's off to the rig. Only at breakfast does Wilf click that his fellow guests in the boarding house – including Izzy's husband Tom – are his colleagues – and superiors. Chris discovers that Wilf comes from a small village in Wales and, much to everyone's amusement, asks him what they do for an idiot when he's not at home. From then on, Wilf becomes known as 'Village'.

And at the heliport, they discover he's done something very idiotic indeed: he's trying to smuggle vodka-injected oranges onto the rig. Chris blows a fuse: alcohol is strictly forbidden offshore. Hilary, while obviously able to take care of herself, is apprehensive. She's going to be the only woman on the *Osprey Explorer* – a rig she already knows is anything but luxurious.

After a long helicopter flight, they arrive at the rig – to discover that a body-bag is waiting to be loaded onto the chopper for the return journey. The body is that of Charlie Macpherson, the mechanic who, they later discover, died whilst watching a pornographic video.

Hilary's arrival causes conflict about cabin allocation. The men sleep four to a cabin while she will have her own. Further consternation arises because no-one wants to sleep in the dead man's bed. Cinders is allocated that bed

Hilary goes through safety drill

and then, already put out by having a woman on the rig, deceives Village and swaps bunks with him.

Tensions escalate when Kevin, the volatile derrickman, accuses the stewards of stealing his wallet and starts a fight with them – a fight eventually stopped by Archie.

Back onshore, the rig superintendent Drew McAllister is in bed with his mistress Tessa Buckingham who has just learned of Charlie Macpherson's demise. A fully-trained mechanic, Tessa is desperate to take his place. Drew will have none of it. Yet Tessa wins the day and bluffs her way into an interview with the director of personnel who 'interviews' her by asking her to mend his garage door. Tessa is livid – but gets the job: the job as one of the few female mechanics in the North Sea.

On the *Osprey Explorer*, a stray rabbit has been discovered in one of the huge drilling pipes just unloaded from the supply vessel. Archie claims the rabbit as his pet, christens it Thumper and, when it later goes missing, goes ballistic. At the same time, Davey, the young roughneck who shares a cabin with Kevin, discovers a spanner under Kevin's bed. Kevin claims it's

for self-protection against the stewards. What it in the end gets used for is for thumping the 'creature' that starts to move under Kevin's sheets. On examination, the creature – now presumed dead – turns out to be Thumper himself. Kevin, appalled by what he has done, dumps the body in a laundry bag.

The stewards – supported by Cinders – then go on strike because of Kevin's behaviour towards them. The near-riot that ensues because of a cancelled breakfast is prevented by Tom Butcher, the admin man and medic, who forces Kevin to apologize.

Hilary is puzzled by the lack of emotion over Charlie Macpherson's death. Ceefax tells her that emotions are feelings and 'why would you want to show them?' It's a sharp lesson to Hilary of the determinedly upbeat, unemotional nature of life offshore.

Village has become prey to much teasing and falls for the ruse of 'putting all the chairs on the heli-deck for Sunday service.' There is no Sunday service – only a helicopter trying to land. The chairs are swiftly removed, the helicopter arrives, and deposits its cargo – Tessa the replacement mechanic.

Tessa is more than a little puzzled by life offshore – not least because of the pandemonium created by Archie who, distraught about the missing Thumper, discovers that Cinders has made rabbit stew for dinner. Eventually placated by the news that 'it was only a joke', Archie is later ecstatic to be reunited with Thumper. One of the stewards has discovered him, now recovered from being knocked out by Kevin, coming down the chute in a laundry bag.

Archie is happy – but the O.I.M. (skipper) Terry Morrell isn't. He knows that the crew are watching a pornographic video in the recreation room. Not an unusual activity, but now Terry has two women on board and he's going to have to do something about it. With Cinders already complaining about women offshore, the last thing he needs is blatant sexism.

Archie, however, is blissfully unaware of what anyone else is doing or thinking. While the others are in the recreation room, he is on the outside of the rig, huddled up against the chill of the night, happily cradling Thumper in his arms – and singing.

Archie and Thumper

EPISODE TWO

A 'mastermind' competition has been organized against a nearby production platform. Some of the crew of the *Osprey Explorer* will fly out to the infinitely more luxurious *Condor* and Ceefax will be pitted against the *Condor*'s resident genius – a bolshie welder known as Joe 90. Ceefax already feels under pressure: his colleagues are placing heavy bets on him.

The departure of Cinders on a three-day survival refresher course coincides with a spell of bad weather and, as no replacement chef can be flown out, Terry asks Tessa to take over as chef. Tessa is furious at this blatant sexism until Terry informs her that, on her CV, it says she used to be a chef. Tessa has forgotten all about that: it was a lie. She refuses Terry's request and Davey, annoyed that she has done so, is rude to her in the canteen. But Tessa holds her own and throws a cup of coffee over him. Davey, being something of a bully, takes his anger out on Village. Ceefax tells Tessa why Davey was rude to her so, much against her will, she takes over the chef's duties.

Tessa's food is disgusting: she even manages to ruin frozen peas. Hilary, thinking she sabotaged the meal to prove a point, congratulates her. Tessa is miffed – she was genuinely trying her best.

Village then comes into his own with the news that he is the son of an Italian chef and no mean cook himself. To everyone's relief, he takes over from Tessa and finally ends all teasing by producing first-class pizzas. At last he has become 'one of the lads' – even if they persist in calling him Village instead of Wilf.

With offshore leave coming up, and with Ian the mechanic and Hilary having discovered many interests in common, Ian asks her to join him on a hillwalking trip. Hilary doesn't give him a definite 'yes' – but nor does she say no.

Ceefax is appalled to discover that his colleagues are banking on winning huge sums on his performance in the mastermind competition against Joe 90. On the *Condor* he freezes, and is incapable of answering a single question. His partner Hilary answers them all but it looks like, in the next round where there are no partners, Joe 90 is going to win.

Back on the *Osprey Explorer*, Drew phones for Tessa. She refuses to speak to him and incurs the wrath of Terry, who, not knowing that she and Drew are having an affair, accuses her of rudeness and insubordination. Eventually she speaks to him and a tearful but inconclusive conversation ensues. Tom – unlike Terry – has put two and two together, and later it becomes apparent that he has used his knowledge of the affair to persuade Tessa to ask Drew a favour. Namely, to persuade him to comply with

Ceefax on the drill floor

Roughnecks

Charlie Macpherson's widow's request to have her husband's ashes scattered at sea from the *Osprey Explorer*. Tessa, at the same time, has told Drew their affair is over.

Ceefax, on the *Condor*, makes a last-minute comeback and defeats Joe 90. His colleagues are delighted and are in ebullient mood when they fly back to the *Osprey Explorer*. A couple of days later, the mood becomes more sombre as Morag Macpherson arrives with her husband's ashes. Yet she also brings something else with her: Kevin's wallet. It transpires that Charlie had found the wallet and, in a telephone conversation with Morag, had explained that he was about to return it – but first he was going to watch a film. He died, of course, watching the film. To spare Morag's feelings, everyone has kept quiet about the nature of that film.

Everyone stands quietly and respectfully as Morag scatters Charlie's ashes from the catwalk of the rig. Tessa, however, is quieter than most. Drew, the last person she wants to see, is on the rig to watch the ceremony.

EPISODE THREE

Terry again sees the men watching pornographic videos. Davey leads him to believe that Village is the importer of the offending material. When questioned by Terry in private, Village refuses to divulge what Terry anyway suspects: that Davey is the culprit.

Half the crew are due for their two weeks offshore. Ian is going hillwalking – with or without Hilary – but before he leaves he confides his worries to Terry about some of the archaic equipment on the *Osprey Explorer* – in particular the outmoded graphite seals used on the mud pumps. Terry later relays this information by phone to Drew – but Drew isn't interested. It's a question, as always, of money.

Onshore, Davey – who has now been reprimanded by Terry about the pornography – picks a fight with Village for sneaking on him. Goaded beyond endurance at the unfair allegation, Village floors Davey and divulges the second secret from his background – he used to be a boxer.

Izzy Butcher outside Morag's house

When he gets to 'Greenacres', Archie is told by Izzy that Jean, his ex-wife, has been involved in an accident and is in hospital. Also at 'Greenacres', Chris gives Izzy's daughter Heather an *Osprey Explorer* sweatshirt and the pair begin to flirt. Tom suspects a burgeoning romance and is not pleased: Chris's reputation isn't exactly spotless and Heather, apart from being Tom's daughter, is only nineteen. The next night, Tom takes Heather out and treats her to dinner – and to a warning about Chris. Annoyed at being treated like a child, Heather denies that she has designs on Chris. Her father, however, is unconvinced.

Archie goes to Glasgow Royal Infirmary to visit Jean and, on seeing her black eye, realizes that she acquired it as a result of a beating by her new husband Bob rather than in a car accident. Driven by the desire to protect both Jean and his children, Archie spends the night in the garden shed of their home. Later, he sees Bob drinking in the garden and, after a tearful conversation with his young daughter who confirms Archie's suspicions about Bob, he later attacks him. Jean, after discharging herself from hospital, stops the fight and tells Archie to mind his own business – she is not coming back to him.

Hilary has decided to accompany Ian on his expedition and, the two of them on his powerful Triumph motorbike, they head off into the Highlands. On their first night they stay in a country house hotel owned by friends of Ian. They are obliged, however, to share a room. Initially reluctant and suspicious, Hilary then realizes that it's too late to look for another hotel so agrees to share – provided that Ian doesn't snore. In the event, it is Hilary who snores ...

The following night, after a blissful day on the hills, their host tells them that a second room is now available. It's evident that both of them would now like to take their relationship further – yet neither is willing to make the move. With a tinge of both embarrassment and regret, they take the extra room.

Back in Aberdeen, Drew McAllister goes to visit Tessa at her flat – only to be told by a neighbour that she's moved out. It is, for Drew, the final and unhappy realization that their affair is definitely over.

Yet where one romance ends, another begins; or at least it would if Heather Butcher could get her way. She follows Chris to a nightclub in Aberdeen and tries to seduce him. Chris reacts to her in the same way as her father: he treats her like a naughty child and tells her to take a taxi home. Yet there is a definite spark of interest and Heather, contrite after her hamfisted attempts at seduction, later apologizes – and asks Chris to give her another chance.

Ian and Heather head off for a weekend in the hills

EPISODE FOUR

Back on the *Osprey Explorer*, Tessa and Ian discover corrosion on one of the rig's winches and report their find to Terry. Acutely aware that his onshore bosses balk at wasting time on unnecessary repairs, Terry examines the corrosion and declares that there is no danger to either man or machinery. He also assures Ian that he would never let the crew work with unsafe machinery.

Later it emerges that the rig hasn't lost a day through either accident or illness for almost twelve months and that, when they reach the twelve-month mark, there will be a bonus for all the crew.

The arrival of Margaret, a female journalist from the *Recorder* then upsets the status quo on the rig. Although everyone knew she was coming, they are all suspicious of what sort of article she intends to write and suspect she is going to opt for the 'sex-starved men' angle. And despite the fact that she is from the 'quality' press, people are worried that she might have got wind of the exact circumstances of Charlie Macpherson's death. Sure enough, she immediately manages to offend Archie and then fires questions at everyone else about life, love, how they cope offshore and what sort of effect their work has on their families. No-one is responsive – least of all Chris, on whom Margaret has evidently set her sights.

One day short of being eligible for their bonuses for uninterrupted work, disaster strikes when Village accidentally drops a heavy box on

Operating the crane

Tessa's foot. It looks like the foot is broken, but everyone puts Tessa under tremendous pressure to keep quiet for a day. Despite being in an enormous amount of pain, Tessa complies.

Back onshore, Heather continues – via the telephone – her pursuit of Chris. She only succeeds, however, in speaking to her father who, aware of how headstrong his daughter can be, realizes that she is completely smitten by Chris – and that she is in danger of neglecting her college education for him.

Yet Chris himself is being relentlessly pursued from another quarter. Margaret, on the pretext of 'research', lures him into the rig's lifeboat. Once there, it becomes evident that her purposes are two-fold: not only is she clearly interested in Chris but she wants him to tell her if the rumours about how Charlie Macpherson died are true. Chris, already annoyed, completely loses his temper when Margaret pulls the lever that lowers the lifeboat. Not only are they now dangling from the side of the rig, but it is impossible to raise the lifeboat from inside. Then, by sheer coincidence, the alarm sounds for a fire drill and, much to the amusement of the rest of the crew, a furious Chris and a now-contrite Margaret are discovered.

In the meantime, Tessa's predicament has also been discovered by Tom. Livid with the others for forcing her to keep quiet, and in his capacity as the rig's medic, he immediately calls a helicopter for Tessa to be taken to hospital. The others, aggrieved that they are going to be deprived of their bonuses, blame Village for their plight. Then Hilary, remembering that the rig was previously working in South East Asia, does a quick calculation. As it crossed the international date line twelve months previously, a day was gained – with the result that it has been operational for three hundred and sixty five days without accident or illness. Tessa's injury, therefore, doesn't jeopardize their bonuses after all. But for Tessa herself it brings a different kind of bonus – a visit, in hospital, from Drew. Despite her resolve to end the affair, she is delighted to see him.

On the rig, Margaret continues in her quest to find out the truth about Charlie Macpherson's death. Collaring Ian, she is again stonewalled. He tries to tell her about the dangers of life offshore but she isn't remotely interested. All she wants is scandal and gossip.

Had she been looking elsewhere, she would have found it. Heather, undaunted her father's angry words on the phone, has sent a letter to Chris. Only on his next period onshore do we realize what it must have contained. Chris is flying out to his house in Spain – but he's not going to be alone. He has succumbed to Heather's protestations of love: she is already in his house when he arrives.

Tom, having recognized Heather's handwriting on the envelope addressed to Chris, is worried. Izzy tells him not to jump to conclusions; that with Heather away at college and Chris in Spain, little harm can come of a letter ...

EPISODE FIVE

Izzy is forced to eat her words when Chris and Heather, now back from Spain, suddenly appear at 'Greenacres'. Tom, Izzy and various members of the rig crew are in the middle of dinner when they arrive and drop their bombshell: they are going to get married.

Chris and Heather

Tom and Izzy are horrified. With Heather being only nineteen, and Chris having a penchant for young girls, Tom in particular assumes that Chris has seduced and probably hoodwinked his daughter – and thumps Chris. A full-scale fight is only averted when the other men, hearing the commotion from the dining room, rush through to restrain Tom.

Chris himself later joins them in the dining room and is met with stony silence and the withdrawal of Archie and Village from the room. Actions speak louder than words and it is clear that they regard Chris as nothing better than a cradle-snatcher.

Later, Chris follows Tom and Cinders to the pub and tries to reason with Tom. But again to no avail: Tom headbutts Chris and hits him so hard that Heather has to take him to hospital.

In other quarters, the path of love is running more smoothly as Tessa and Drew get back together. Their lovemaking, however, is interrupted by a phonecall from Drew's unsuspecting wife. It's clear that Drew is going to have to do something about the situation; the strain of deception is beginning to get to him.

At 'Greenacres', Ceefax tells Cinders and Archie that they ought at least to try to be civil to Chris. They remain unconvinced. Heather, meanwhile, is trying the same tactic with her father. Yet Tom remains unyielding and Heather finally loses her temper. She storms off, saying that he has no business telling her how to run her life when he himself has been absent on the rig for half of that life.

As they prepare to go back offshore the next day, Tessa tells Hilary that her affair with Drew has started again and that Drew has told her he is going to leave his wife. Furthermore, he will be coming out to the rig with them to check out Ian's repeated complaints about safety. On the rig, Ian himself later tells Hilary that he's going to pack in his job as an offshore mechanic. Hilary is distraught.

Late at night and in the middle of a storm, there is a problem on the drill floor. The engine-cooling pump is losing pressure and the crew – mechanics Ian and Tessa in particular – have to battle to save the generator from overheating. Despite their efforts, the power fails and the rig is plunged into darkness. Although the back-up generator later goes into operation, the malfunctioning pump and loss of pressure has caused another problem: the well below them is in danger of blowing. The alarm sounds and they hear the words that all rig crews dread: 'This is not a drill. Repeat. This is not a drill.'

A helicopter is called and those not currently on duty are to be the first evacuees. Amongst them are Tessa and Ian (whose shifts have just finished), Hilary, Drew, Archie and Village. Donning survival suits, they rush through the rain onto the heli-deck and seconds later the helicopter is airborne. Mere seconds after that, Chris manages to solve the pressure problem – but not before a jet of mud shoots in the direction of the helicopter. Suddenly the helicopter lurches out of control – and plunges into the turbulent North Sea.

Those on the rig watch in horror as the helicopter disappears, while its passengers fight against mounting panic and to free themselves from the stricken aircraft as it floats upside down in the sea.

Lifeboats are immediately lowered. Even in their survival suits, the passengers' chances of lasting more than a few minutes in the sea are slim. Some of them, however, have managed to free themselves and to reach the surface. The lifeboats pick up the survivors and then search frantically in the darkness for those still missing. The last sound is of Hilary shouting hysterically for one of them: Ian.

Terry in action

EPISODE SIX

Two bodies have been recovered from the helicopter crash. One person, however, is still missing. It is Ian, and a distraught Hilary has refused to leave the rig with the other survivors. Eventually, Ceefax has to give her drugged coffee in order to make her sleep so they can get her back onshore.

Ceefax has no qualms about doing that, but he does have a problem about what he sees as the cause of the crash. He reckons it was Chris's fault – and tells him so. He is sure that Chris, in preventing the well blowing, opened the wrong mud diverter, causing mud to spatter all over the heli-deck and over the windscreen of the helicopter itself.

Terry and the survivors of the crash are all questioned about the accident and Ceefax wrestles with his conscience – especially as everyone else, now gathered at 'Greenacres', has got wind of what Chris may or may not have done. They put pressure on Ceefax to come clean and eventually he does – to the accident investigators. To his immense relief, they tell him that Chris has already told them about the mud diverter. They, in turn, told him that it didn't cause the accident. Ceefax later tells the others that they have all misjudged Chris. They have no choice but to agree.

Ian's body is found that day and his possessions returned to Izzy at

'Greenacres'. Amongst them is Ian's favourite tape: a compilation of the hits of The Incredible String Band. The evening turns into something of a wake for Ian as, Hilary included, they drink whisky and reminisce. The only people missing are Chris and Heather: only Izzy knows that they are to be married the next day at what turns out to be the quietest wedding ever. It takes place in a registry office with no friends or family present.

Izzy and Tom at the wedding

Yet because Chris's name has been cleared and because everybody belatedly realizes they have been less than charitable to the engaged couple, when Izzy lets slip where they are they all drive out to the hotel where Heather and Chris are spending their honeymoon. Chris is initially alarmed to see Tom, but the latter grits his teeth and wishes him well – and tells him to look after Heather. At that point everyone enters the hotel and the occasion turns into a surprise wedding reception. To add a poignant note, the hotel is the same one that Ian and Hilary frequented – and the music the band plays is that of The Incredible String Band.

All is well – until a still-taciturn Tom announces to Izzy that he wants to quit working offshore. Izzy is stunned: for twenty years they have lived two weeks together and two weeks apart, while taking most decisions together. Izzy has learned to like things that way. She's none too keen on Tom taking a unilateral decision. Furthermore, she isn't sure how their marriage will work if they are going to be together all the time ...

Credits

Roughnecks 1

Produced by	Moira Williams
	Charles Elton
Directed by	Sandy Johnson
Written by	Kieran Prendiville
Title Music by	Mike Post
Music by	Mike Post & Roger Neill

Main cast

Tessa	Teresa Banham
Ceefax	Colum Convey
Ian	Paul Copley
Tom	James Cosmo
Chris	Liam Cunningham
Hilary	Francesca Hunt
Heather	Ashley Jensen
Terry	Bruce Jones
Drew	John McGlynn
Izzy	Annie Raitt
Kevin	George Rossi
Archie	Clive Russell
Wilf	Hywel Simons
Cinders	Ricky Tomlinson
Davey	Alec Westwood

Developed by	Kieran Prendiville
Consultants	Jonathan Cullen
	Peter Searles
Script Editor	Sue Hogg
Casting Advisor	Gail Stevens
Casting Assistant	Andy Pryor
First Assistant Director	Francesco Reidy
Second Assistant Director	Brian Binns
Third Assistant Director	Amanda Stevens
Production Runner	Tillie Williams

Production Runner	Dawn Harvey
Production Co-Ordinator	Deryn Stafford
Production Secretary	Sam Mitchell
Script Supervisor	Liz West
Focus Puller	Mary Kyte
Clapper Loader	Daniel Cohen
Grips	Tex Childs
	John Phillips
Gaffer	Keith Woodward
Best Boy	Dave Owen
Steadicam Operator	Simon Bray
Underwater Cameraman	Steve Foote
Special Effects Supervisor	Peter Hutchinson
Sound Recordist	Bruce White
Boom Operator	Terry Sharratt
Location Manager	Sue Quinn
Locations Assistant	Michael Harm
Art Director	Mark Raggett
Design Assistant	Julian Ashby
Construction Manager	Malcolm Roberts
Production Buyer	Mike Smith
Property Master	Graeme Purdy
Location Propmaster	Ray Perry
Stand-by Props	Nick Milner
Wardrobe Supervisor	Verity Hawkes
Wardrobe Assistant	Jo Rickard
Make-up Design	Jenny Boost
Make-Up Assistant	Norma Webb
Dubbing Mixer	Dave Humphries
Dubbing Editor	Kevin Brazier
Assistant Film Editor	Kate Fairservice
Graphics	Pat Gavin
Production Accountant	Freya Pinsent
Assistant Accountant	Carin Mistry
Production Executive	Jill Pack

The Producers would like to acknowledge the
assistance of the RGIT Survival Centre Ltd,
Aberdeen

Associate Producer..........................Barney Reisz
Costume Designer......................Howard Burden
Production Designer ....Tim Hutchinson
Film Editors ....Don Fairservice
Amanda Smith
Tim Hands
Director of Photography.....................John Daly
Executive Producer.................Michael Wearing
A First Choice Production for BBC
© BBC MCMXCIV

Supporting Cast

Episode 1

RGIT Instructor ....Gilly Gilchrist
Students ....Aidan Watts
Jason Barry
Policeman ....Arturo Venegas
Peter ....Craig Hemmings
Helen................................Lorraine Hemmings
Jean ....Deborah Maclaren
Bob..Seamus O'Neill
Bernadette ....Sharon Small
Callum...Colin Brown
Woman in taxi ....Annie Inglis
Check-in girl.................................Katy Murphy
Carole............................Frances Carrigan
Storeman......................................Bill Dick
Admin man ....Tony Nyland
George ....Tam White
Morag ....Juliet Cadzow
Norsco receptionist..........................Aline Mowat
Denness...................................Ron Donachie
Telegram Sam ....John Kazek

Episode 2

Security guard..............................Mark Sangster
Telegram Sam ....John Kazek

Morag ....Juliet Cadzow
John ....Ian McNeice
Joe 90 ....Ben Mendelsohn
Joe 90's mates ....David Y Cheung
Stig Rossen
Carole....................................Frances Carrigan

Episode 3

George ....Tam White
Norsco Receptionist........................Aline Mowat
Jean ....Deborah Maclaren
Jake ....Angus McInnes
Bob..Seamus O'Neill
Helen............................Lorraine Hemmings
Neighbour ....Joy McBrinn
RGIT Instructor ....Gilly Gilchrist
Morag ....Juliet Cadzow

Episode 4

Margaret ....Race Davies
Telegram Sam ....John Kazek

Episode 5

Barman ....Jamie Adair
Nurse...Morag Hepburn
Clergyman ....James Bryce
Carole....................................Frances Carrigan
Telegram Sam ....John Kazek
Rescuer...Alan Stuart
Stunts ....Paul Heasman
Sy Holland

Episode 6

Telegram Sam ....John Kazek
Carole....................................Frances Carrigan
Newscaster ....Sally Ann Burnett
Burgess..Bruce Jamieson
Melling..................................David Bannerman
Phillips ....Benny Young
Witness......................................Kenneth Owens
Jake ....Angus McInnes
Wedding band ....Mike Heron

ACKNOWLEDGEMENTS

TERESA BANHAM
COLUM CONVEY
PAUL COPLEY
JAMES COSMO
LIAM CUNNINGHAM
CHARLES ELTON
KEN HODCROFT
FRANCESCA HUNT
ASHLEY JENSEN
SANDY JOHNSON
BRUCE JONES
JOHN McGLYNN
SAM MITCHELL
ROGER NEILL
FREYA PINSENT
KIERAN PRENDIVILLE
ANNIE RAITT
GEORGE ROSSI
CLIVE RUSSELL
HYWEL SIMONS
RICKY TOMLINSON
ALEC WESTWOOD
MOIRA WILLIAMS
DAVID WILSON